1st EDITION

Perspectives on Modern World History

The Attack on Pearl Harbor

1st EDITION

Perspectives on Modern World History

The Attack on Pearl Harbor

David Haugen and Susan Musser

Book Editors

GREENHAVEN PRESS
A part of Gale, Cengage Learning

GALE
CENGAGE Learning

Detroit • New York • San Francisco • New Haven, Conn • Waterville, Maine • London

Christine Nasso, *Publisher*
Elizabeth Des Chenes, *Managing Editor*

For product information and technology assistance, contact us at
Gale Customer Support, 1-800-877-4253.

For permission to use material from this text or product, submit all requests online at
www.cengage.com/permissions.

Further permissions questions can be e-mailed to permissionrequest@cengage.com.

Articles in Greenhaven Press anthologies are often edited for length to meet page requirements. In addition, original titles of these works are changed to clearly present the main thesis and to explicitly indicate the author's opinion. Every effort is made to ensure that Greenhaven Press accurately reflects the original intent of the authors. Every effort has been made to trace the owners of copyrighted material.

Cover image Custom Medical Stock Photo, Inc. Reproduced by permission.

LIBRARY OF CONGRESS CATALOGING-IN-PUBLICATION DATA

The attack on Pearl Harbor / David Haugen and Susan Musser, book editors.
    p. cm. -- (Perspectives on modern world history)
  Includes bibliographical references and index.
  ISBN 978-0-7377-5004-1 (hardcover)
  1. Pearl Harbor (Hawaii), Attack on, 1941--Juvenile literature. I. Haugen, David M., 1969- II. Musser, Susan.
  D767.92.A788 2011
  940.54'26693--dc22

                                                                        2010033590

Printed in the United States of America
2 3 4 5 6 7 14 13 12 11

CONTENTS

President Roosevelt addresses Congress, petitioning the legislators to declare a state of war against Japan in response to the surprise attack against the Hawaiian base and other U.S. holdings in the Pacific.

the Roosevelt administration knowingly and deliberately concocted a plan to blame the extensive casualties and destruction at Pearl Harbor on the military commanders at the base.

Pearl Harbor. He maintains that the commanders at the Hawaiian base had received enough warnings from Washington to have prepared better for imminent attack.

FOREWORD

"History cannot give us a program for the future, but it can give us a fuller understanding of ourselves, and of our common humanity, so that we can better face the future."
—Robert Penn Warren,
American poet and novelist

The history of each nation is punctuated by momentous events that represent turning points for that nation, with an impact felt far beyond its borders. These events—displaying the full range of human capabilities, from violence, greed, and ignorance to heroism, courage, and strength—are nearly always complicated and multifaceted. Any student of history faces the challenge of grasping the many strands that constitute such world-changing events as wars, social movements, and environmental disasters. But understanding these significant historic events can be enhanced by exposure to a variety of perspectives, whether of people involved intimately or of ones observing from a distance of miles or years. Understanding can also be increased by learning about the controversies surrounding such events and exploring hot-button issues from multiple angles. Finally, true understanding of important historic events involves knowledge of the events' human impact—of the ways such events affected people in their everyday lives—all over the world.

Perspectives on Modern World History examines global historic events from the twentieth-century onward by presenting analysis and observation from numerous vantage points. Each volume offers high school, early college level, and general interest readers a thematically arranged anthology of previously published materials that address a major historical event, with an emphasis on international coverage. Each volume opens with background information on the event, then presents the controversies surrounding that event, and concludes with first-person narratives from people who lived through the event or were affected by it. By providing primary sources from the time of the event, as well as relevant commentary surrounding the event, this series can be used to inform debate, help develop critical thinking skills, increase global awareness, and enhance an understanding of international perspectives on history.

Material in each volume is selected from adiverse range of sources, including journals, magazines, newspapers, nonfiction books, personal narratives, speeches, congressional testimony, government documents, pamphlets, organization newsletters, and position papers Articles taken from these sources are carefully edited and introduced to provide context and background. Each volume of Perspectives on Modern World History includes an array of views on events of global significance. Much of the material comes from international sources and from U.S. sources that provide extensive international coverage.

Each volume in the Perspectives on Modern World History series also includes:

- A full-color **world map**, offering context and geographic perspective.
- An annotated **table of contents** that provides a brief summary of each essay in the volume.
- An **introduction** specific to the volume topic.
- For each viewpoint, a brief **introduction** that has notes about the author and source of the viewpoint, and that provides a summary of its main points.
- Full-color **charts**, **graphs**, **maps**, and other visual representations.

- Informational **sidebars** that explore the lives of key individuals, give background on historical events, or explain scientific or technical concepts.
- A **glossary** that defines key terms, as needed.
- A **chronology** of important dates preceding, during, and immediately following the event.
- A **bibliography** of additional books, periodicals, and Web sites for further research.
- A comprehensive **subject index** that offers access to people, places, and events cited in the text.

Perspectives on Modern World History is designed for a broad spectrum of readers who want to learn more about not only history but also current events, political science, government, international relations, and sociology—students doing research for class assignments or debates, teachers and faculty seeking to supplement course materials, and others wanting to improve their understanding of history. Each volume of Perspectives on Modern World History is designed to illuminate a complicated event, to spark debate, and to show the human perspective behind the world's most significant happenings of recent decades.

INTRODUCTION

The United States' involvement in World War II did not begin with the Japanese raid on Pearl Harbor on December 7, 1941. By that infamous date, the U.S. had become enmeshed economically, if not always politically, in the conflicts that were playing out in both Europe and Asia. President Franklin Delano Roosevelt's administration—which presided over the bulk of the war years—had already committed to aid nations that were victims of aggression by the Axis powers, namely, Germany, Japan, Italy, and its allies. After the Japanese invaded China in 1937, for example, the U.S. government began loaning the Chinese government money to fulfill wartime production contracts. In 1940, a year after war broke out in Europe and a time when Britain and her commonwealth satellites were struggling alone against the onslaught of Nazi Germany, Roosevelt brokered deals with London to supply the British government with arms to carry on the fight. In September of that year, the two countries forged an agreement in which the U.S. gave fifty naval destroyers to the U.K. in exchange for the right to build naval and air bases in Canada and British possessions in the Caribbean.

In March of 1941, Roosevelt instigated a broader plan to help the Allies—the nations fighting the Axis powers. Called the Lend-Lease Act, the new program stipulated that the President "may, from time to time, when he deems it in the interest of national defense, authorize the Secretary of War, the Secretary of the Navy, or the head of any other department or agency of the Government . . . to sell, transfer title to, exchange, lease, lend, or otherwise dispose of, to any such government any defense article [manufactured in government arsenals, factories, or shipyards]." Under the act, just over $50 billion in war materials were shipped to England, Russia, China, and France in trade for goods and land rights, or with long-term repayment agreements. The Lend-Lease Act was part of Roosevelt's mission to turn the United States into "the great arsenal of democracy" and, in his words, "eliminate the dollar sign" from international trade that would help the European Allies stand up to Adolf Hitler. The German chancellor even recognized this deal as an aggressive act and gave German submarines permission to prey on U.S. ships suspected of carrying war supplies to England.

The Lend-Lease Act was adopted not only because Roosevelt was partial to the Allied cause but also because by 1940 the U.S. public's sympathies favored those who were fighting fascism. Such bias was not clear-cut in the decades preceding the war, however. After World War I, the majority of Americans believed that the government should stay out of foreign wars. Conservative elements—especially in rural and small-town America—argued that the country was facing its own troubles enduring the hardships of the Great Depression; most, in fact, called for a reduction in arms as a way of keeping the national debt down during the hard economic times. In 1935, fifty thousand veterans marched through Washington, D.C., in support of continued peace and in opposition to any intervention in European affairs.

At nearly the same time, though, Roosevelt was drafting a "peace" plan that enlisted strong European powers such as France, England, and Russia to compel Hitler to demilitarize or face the might of a unified blockade of goods to Germany. "If this did not succeed," Roosevelt predicted, "the chances are we will have a world war." The president was not eager for war, but he was not ignorant of the fact that a European conflict would likely extend beyond the borders of that continent and put U.S. interests at risk. Within five years, these prospects seemed realized. The government recognized that Nazi Germany, which was already steamrolling France and the Low Countries (Belgium, the Netherlands, and Luxembourg), had begun rousing subversive elements in Mexico and Central and South America. Fearing the overthrow of regimes so close to U.S. borders, the President flexed a limited amount of military muscle in the region and reinforced friendly diplomacy with threatened Latin American governments.

The administration also had to contend with Japan's expansionist policies in the Pacific. While already supplying China with capital, Roosevelt's government hoped to prevent Japan from seizing the French and Dutch colonies in Southeast Asia, which were now isolated thanks to Hitler's victories in Europe. In July 1940, the U.S. government issued an embargo against Japan that ended the sale of scrap metal and gasoline to Japan. Though feeling the loss of these needed military supplies, Japan ignored the embargo and, in July 1941, moved into French Indochina (which includes modern-day Laos, Cambodia, and parts of Vietnam) to grab natural resources and open another front on China. The Roosevelt administration immediately responded by freezing Japanese assets in the United States. Clearly, diplomacy between the two powers was failing. In a May 1, 2006, article for the *Freeman*, historian Robert Higgs claimed, "Roosevelt and his subordinates knew they were putting Japan in an untenable position and that the Japanese government might well try to escape the stranglehold by going to war."

Higgs is one of many historians who believe Franklin Roosevelt cornered the Japanese into doing what Germany would not—conducting a military strike against a U.S. target that would force the United States to become an open participant in the expanding global war. Whether or not this was the case, the president had less to fear from an isolationist public on the eve of war than he had in earlier years. The steadfastness of the British people, who endured the German aerial blitz that began in 1940, won the hearts of most Americans, and various filmmakers were openly mocking Hitler and his empire-building on the big screen. In 1941, the American Volunteer Group (a unit composed of volunteer crewmen from the U.S. military) began earning praise in the press for its successful "freelance" operations in China against the Japanese, revealing that the United States was already participating in the fight against tyranny. Indeed, even though Americans predominantly did not want to be enmeshed in another war, it was clear to them that if events compelled mobilization, there was no doubt which side the United States would join.

On December 7, 1941, Japanese dive-bombers and torpedo planes left their carriers roughly 230 miles north of the Hawaiian island of Oahu and proceeded to attack Pearl Harbor, where the bulk of the United States' Pacific fleet lay at anchor. Thirty minutes before the attack, the Japanese cut off diplomatic contact with the United States. The U.S. government recognized the significance of this sudden communication blackout, but by then the course of events was unstoppable. Two waves of Japanese planes struck the major capital ships and airbases at Pearl Harbor. Of the eight battleships tied up at dock, four were sunk and the others were damaged. One hundred eighty-eight U.S. aircraft were destroyed on runways, in hangars, or in the air. More than 2,400 personnel lost their lives—1,177 of them on the USS *Arizona*. That renowned battleship suffered the most damage when its ammunition magazine exploded, tearing apart the ship and leaving fires burning for two days after the attack.

The Japanese raid was a striking success, crippling the U.S. fleet and allowing Japan to continue its conquests in the Pacific unhindered. An official declaration of war did not accompany the raid, but the Japanese government printed one that reached Washington the next day. The Roosevelt administration declared war on Japan on December 9, 1941, as well. Three days later, Germany declared war on the United States, and the remnants of U.S. isolationism faded away. The U.S. was now firmly involved in the conflict that stretched across all parts of the globe.

In the aftermath of Pearl Harbor, the United States had to mobilize for the war it had dreaded. Despite the growing partisanship for the Allied cause, the American military was only slowly building up its martial capacities. In 1939 and 1940, Roosevelt had begun to call for the building of more military aircraft, the creation of a War Resources Board, and the imposition of a military draft. While there was resistance to some of these measures, the U.S. government was able to increase military spending in the years preceding its official entry into the war because the isolationists conceded that the nation needed to ensure its own defense and military leaders agreed. "The Army still saw its role as protecting the United States and the Western Hemisphere from hostile European forces rather than participating in global coalition warfare," the U.S. Army Center of Military History report on mobilization stated in its 1999 retrospective overview of mobilization. Once war was declared, however, the military branches got a boost in enlistment as hundreds of thousands of eager young men and women signed up to fight for their country, and the War Department immediately adopted plans to increase the production of munitions, warships, tanks, cannons, and aircraft.

With this fervor, the United States' Army and Navy were expected to go on the offensive. But by then Hitler's Europe was a wall that could not be breached, and large-scale invasion was not an option for the under-strength U.S. military. Besides, most Americans wanted revenge against the Japanese for their sneak attack, and military leaders feared that if the United States didn't confront Japanese expansion in the Pacific, U.S. possessions in the region (such as the Philippines, Guam, Midway, and Wake Island) would quickly fall. However, with the bulk of its fleet destroyed or damaged, the United States' range of action was limited. Fortunately, the U.S. aircraft carriers in the Pacific were on maneuvers during the raid on Pearl Harbor and had thus escaped the battle. In a Joint Chiefs of Staffs meeting in the White House on December 21, 1941, President Roosevelt asked that the military devise a reprisal that would involve the bombing of Japan in order to lower Japanese morale and lift the American mood. A plan was quickly developed to utilize a U.S. carrier to launch heavy bombers against Tokyo and a few seaport cities. The famed Doolittle Raid, named after its commander Lieutenant Colonel James Doolittle, occurred on April 18, 1942, and proved a success in raising American spirits even though the damage the bombers inflicted was minimal.

These actions by the United States, however, did not alter the course of Japanese expansion. By the time Roosevelt had called for the bombing of Japan, Japanese marines had already invaded the Philippines and seized Guam, and by the end of December 1941, the Philippines were beginning to weaken, Wake Island succumbed, and the British lost Hong Kong and their share of Borneo to skillfully conducted Japanese attacks. The numerous Japanese victories helped spur Roosevelt to enact Executive Order 9066 in February 1942—an order that mandated the removal of Japanese Americans and Japanese nationals from strategic areas of the west coast of the U.S. for fear of sabotage or other subversive actions. Despite such precautions and the still-undefeated carrier fleet, the United States would not gain the upper hand in the Pacific until June 1942, when a Japanese carrier squadron and its attendant invasion force was thwarted from seizing Midway Island, which is only 1,300 miles from Oahu. From that point on, the U.S. and the Allies fought a protracted campaign to retake lost possessions in the Pacific. The Japanese were skilled fighters and did not yield ground easily. Only after years of bloody combat did the Japanese empire shrink as southeast Asia was retaken and one after another Japanese-held island fell to Allied manpower. On August 6 and 9, 1945, President Harry S. Truman, Roosevelt's successor, signed the order allowing U.S. bombers to drop atomic weapons on the Japanese cities of Hiroshima and Nagasaki. The Pacific war which, for the United States, began with a bombing subsequently ended with a bombing. As Truman remarked in his first official statement after the atomic attacks, "The Japanese began the war from the air at Pearl Harbor. They have been repaid manyfold."

World Map

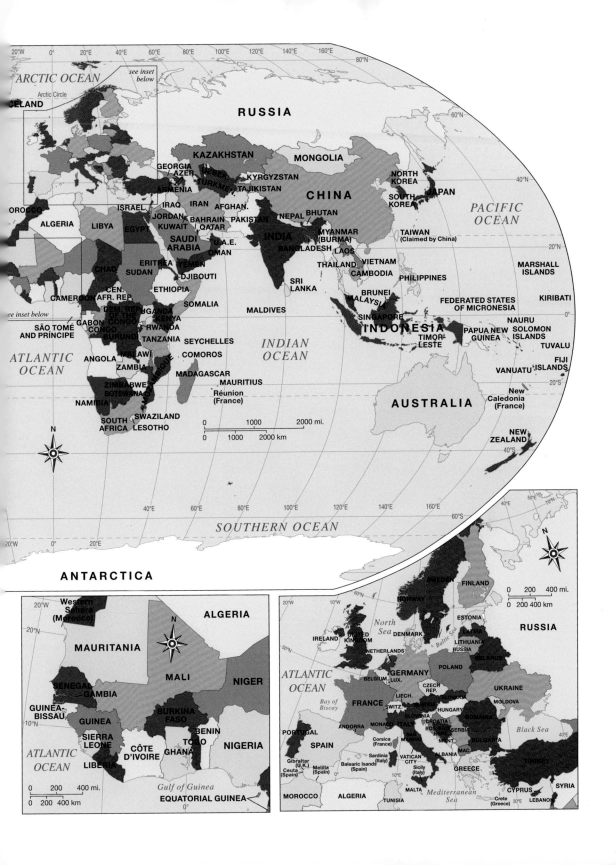

CHAPTER 1

Historical Background on the Attack on Pearl Harbor

The Attack on Pearl Harbor

Michael J. O'Neal

In the following viewpoint, Michael J. O'Neal provides an over-view of the attack on Pearl Harbor on December 7, 1941. O'Neal asserts that Japan, humiliated by its lack of prosperity and status in the years following World War I, gave way to milita-rism among its leadership. These leaders convinced the nation that Japan's rise would derive from expansion into southeast Asia and the Pacific where resources such as oil and rubber lay. In order to accomplish this, Japan had to interrupt the United States' efforts to aid China and other Asian nations, O'Neal writes. The Japanese military hoped a sudden, quick blow at the U.S. fleet at Pearl Harbor would keep the United States from thwarting Japan's expansion plans, and on December 7 launched carrier-based aircraft two hundred miles from Pearl Harbor to carry out a daring raid that crippled the United States' surface fleet. O'Neal comments that the success of the raid was all the more remarkable because various sources had hinted to the U.S. government that an attack was imminent,

Photo on previous page: On December 7, 1941, the Japanese military conducted a bombing raid on the U.S. military base at Pearl Harbor, Hawaii. The USS *West Virginia* was one of many navy ships destroyed. (**AP Images.**)

SOURCE. Michael J. O'Neal, *Encyclopedia of Espionage, Intelligence and Security*. Detroit, MI: 2004. © 2004 by Gale. Reproduced by per-mission of Gale, a part of Cengage Learning.

yet little was done to rouse the fleet or prepare for the coming battle. Michael J. O'Neal is a former literature teacher who now writes for several educational publishing houses.

On December 7, 1941, Japanese military forces attacked the United States naval fleet anchored at Pearl Harbor on the Hawaiian island of Oahu. The surprise attack nearly devastated the American Pacific fleet. Three cruisers, three destroyers, and eight battleships along "Battleship Row" were severely damaged, and two battleships, the *Oklahoma* and the *Arizona*, were sunk. Additionally, nearly 350 American warplanes on Oahu were destroyed, virtually all that were on the ground. Over 2,400 U.S. servicemen lost their lives, and nearly 1,200 were wounded. The success of the daring attack severely impaired America's ability to check the expansion of the Japanese empire in the Pacific during the first years of WWII.

Japan Seeks to Assert Its Power in World Affairs

As an island nation, Japan had developed a rich and complex social structure. It resisted westernization by sealing itself off from contact with the outside world, particularly Europe and the United States. By the early twentieth century, though, Japan's efforts to achieve self-sufficiency were failing, for the nation lacked its own raw materials and other resources. Some members of the ruling class argued that Japan could grow and prosper only by modernizing and adopting Western technology. Japanese nationalists, though, advocated a different path: the establishment of an empire that would not only elevate Japan's stature

> [Japan's] Samurai believed that in the peace negotiations following [World War I] the United States and Great Britain had treated Japan as a second-class nation.

in the eyes of the world but also guarantee access to the resources the nation needed. Moreover, many members of the nation's traditional warrior class—the Samurai—were embittered by the aftermath of World War I. Japan had backed the victorious Allies, but the Samurai believed that in the peace negotiations following the war the United States and Great Britain had treated Japan as a second-class nation. They, too, longed to assert Japan's place in world affairs.

Japan began to flex its muscles in 1931. Japanese forces stationed in Manchuria, northeast of China, to protect a Japanese railway that transported goods and raw materials out of the country suddenly seized control of all of Manchuria. Then in 1937, Japanese forces attacked the eastern provinces of China, seizing China's capital, Nanking, and the old capital, Beijing, in brutal fashion. Observers in the West were horrified by reports of the atrocities against civilians committed by Japanese invaders in the so-called "Rape of Nanking." Under the leadership of Minister of War Hideki Tojo, Japan's objective was to establish a defensive perimeter—the "Greater East Asia Co-Prosperity Sphere"—in the western Pacific. This perimeter was to extend from the Jurile Islands northeast of Japan, south to the Marianas and Marshall Islands, west through the Solomon Islands, New Guinea, and the East Indies, then northward into the Indian Ocean and southeast Asia. Tojo believed that Japan could thus drive out the Western powers, achieve a position of preeminence in East Asia, and free the nation from its dependence on Western oil, coal, rubber, ore, and other vital resources.

Tojo's strategy, however, was bringing him ever closer to conflict with those powers. The Dutch, for example, controlled the East Indies, France had a presence in Indo-China, the United States controlled the Philippines, and Malaya was a British colony. Concerned about Japanese aggression, Holland, Great Britain, and the United States

imposed a trade embargo on Japan on July 26, 1941, cutting off supplies of resources to the increasingly belligerent nation. Tojo, now prime minister, was convinced that the West's goal was to starve Japan into submission.

Events came to a boil in September, 1941. United States Secretary of State Cordell Hull demanded that Japan withdraw its troops from China and Southeast Asia. While many Japanese military leaders quailed at the prospect of going to war with the United States, Tojo convinced them that acceding to American demands would be a humiliating diplomatic defeat. While carrying on protracted—and deceptive—negotiations with the United States, Japan invaded Thailand, Malaya, Burma, and the East Indies. And on November 26, the Japanese navy set sail for Pearl Harbor, where most of the U.S. Pacific fleet was docked.

> "Because it was Sunday morning, most of the U.S. naval personnel were ashore, and most of the antiaircraft defenses were unmanned [at Pearl Harbor]."

An Attack in Two Waves

Traveling under strict radio silence and screened from view by a large weather front, the Japanese battle fleet—six aircraft carriers, two battleships, two cruisers, and nine destroyers—remained undetected until it came within two hundred miles of the Hawaiian Islands. On the morning of December 7, 183 torpedo bombers and dive-bombers took off from the aircraft carriers. The Japanese pilots knew exactly where they were going because spies on the islands had given them elaborate and detailed scale models of the base, including Battleship Row. Because it was Sunday morning, most of the U.S. naval personnel were ashore, and most of the antiaircraft defenses were unmanned. At 7:49 A.M. local time, the attack began—and by 8:12 much of the fleet had been damaged or sunk. A second wave of bombers arrived at nine o'clock to finish what the first wave had started. In a little more than an hour, the United States fleet was severely crippled. Two days later, on December 9, the United States declared war on Japan. . . .

Photo on previous page: Minister of War Hideki Tojo was instrumental in convincing other Japanese military leaders to go to war with the United States. (Time & Life Pictures/Getty Images.)

Admiral Yamamoto Gives the Order to Attack Pearl Harbor

On July 25, 1941, U.S. President Franklin D. Roosevelt froze Japanese assets in retaliation for its occupation of southern Indochina, a move that severed all trade between the two nations. Now Japan's ever-precious supply of oil was cut off, causing it to seek domination of the petroleum-rich Dutch East Indies and to risk war with the United States and Britain. In late September, Admiral Isoroku Yamamoto visited Admiral Nagano Osami, chief of the naval general staff, to dissuade him from pursuing military plans made on September 6 to fight the United States. If war, however, was truly inevitable, Japan—Yamamoto said—should scrap traditional plans centering on lying in wait for the American battle fleet and ambushing it near Japan itself. Rather than allow a U.S. build-up, Japan must make a preemptive strike, crippling the American navy at the outset of the conflict. Such a move could shift the strategic balance in Japan's favor, protect the all-important southern flank in

Warnings of an Impending Attack

A question that continues to intrigue historians is how American intelligence could have failed so spectacularly, given the circumstances. The diplomatic situation was tense, and growing tenser. It was known that Germany, a Japanese ally, was pressing Japan to take action to divert American attention away from Europe. As early as January 27, 1941, Joseph Grew, the U.S. ambassador in Japan, reported to Secretary of State Hull that the embassy had learned from Japanese sources that a mass attack on Pearl Harbor was planned in case hostilities broke out. The United States had broken the Japanese dip-

> On the morning of December 7, Army Chief of Staff General George C. Marshall sent an urgent warning to commanders in the Pacific that intercepted Japanese diplomatic messages strongly suggested an attack was imminent.

southeast Asia, and hopefully lead to a negotiated peace.

Yamamoto's plan eventually called for a massive air strike involving all six large carriers of the First Air Fleet; they had to approach within 200 miles of Hawaii without being discovered. On December 1, Japan's highest decision-making body, the Imperial Conference, decided upon war with the United States, Britain, and the Netherlands. Emperor Hirohito personally issued the orders to Yamamoto: "You must be determined to meet our expectations by exalting our force and authority throughout the world by annihilating the enemy." Aboard his flagship *Yamato*, stationed in Japan's Inland Sea, Yamamoto gave the coded attack orders to his strike force: "Climb Mount Niitaka," a reference to a peak in Formosa that was the highest point in the Japanese empire.

SOURCE. *"Isoroku Yamamoto,"* Encyclopedia of World Biography, *2nd ed. 17 Vols. Gale Research, 1998.*

lomatic code (called Purple), so war planners from the president on down knew that spies had been reporting on the fleet deployment in Hawaii. In the weeks and days before the attack, encrypted diplomatic traffic became heavier, and increasingly ominous. On November 19, for example, American codebreakers intercepted a message from Tokyo to diplomatic posts in Washington, D.C., and several West Coast cities. The message instructed these offices to destroy all codes, coding machines, papers, and the like if they heard the words "East Wind Rain" (*Higashi No Kazeame*) in the daily weather forecast. On Thursday, December 4, the United States intercepted the so-called "winds message." Even on the morning of December 7, Army Chief of Staff General George C. Marshall sent an urgent warning to commanders in the Pacific that intercepted Japanese diplomatic messages strongly suggested

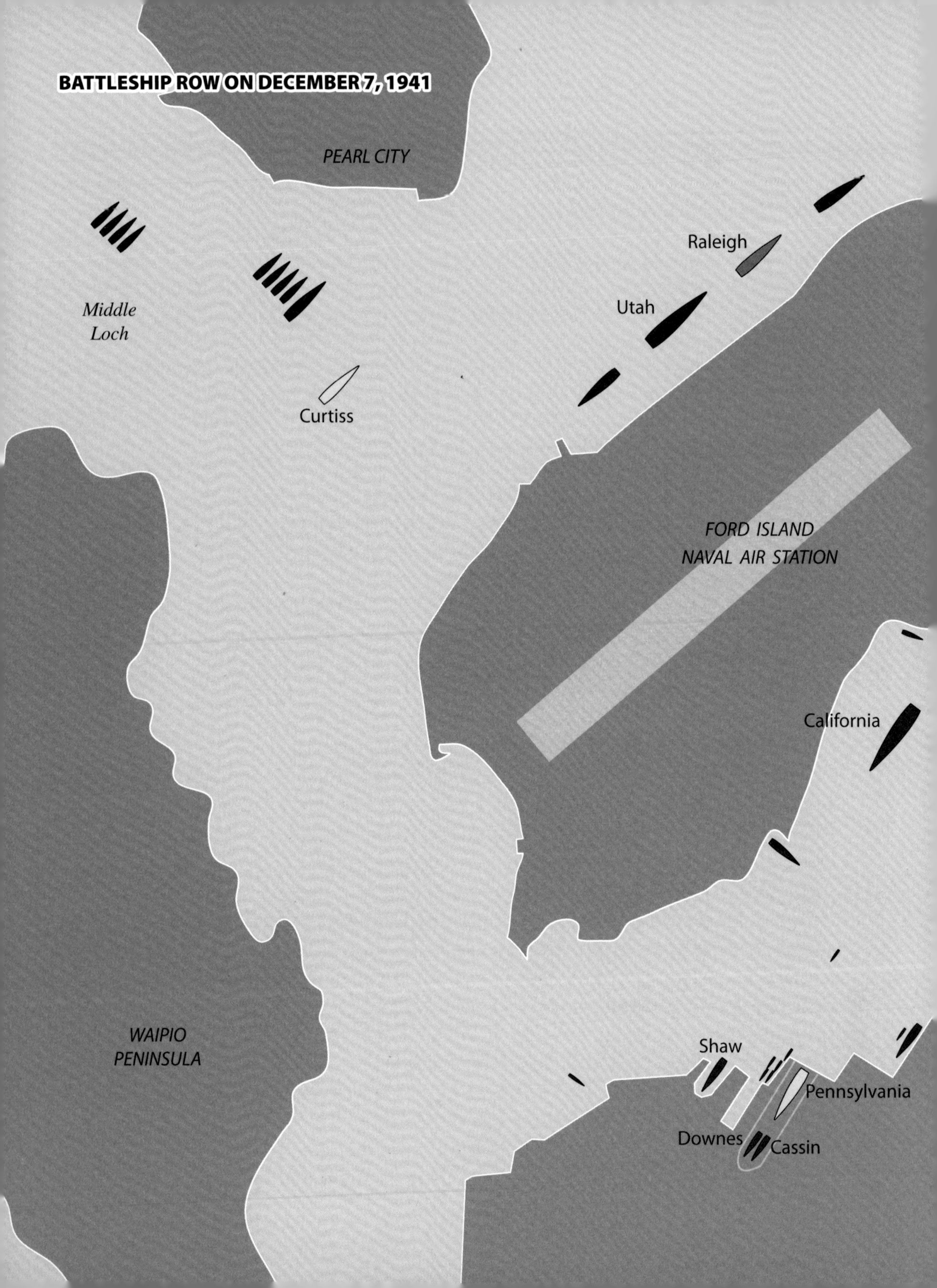

BATTLESHIP ROW ON DECEMBER 7, 1941

PEARL CITY

Middle
Loch

Curtiss

Raleigh

Utah

FORD ISLAND
NAVAL AIR STATION

California

WAIPIO
PENINSULA

Shaw

Pennsylvania

Downes   Cassin

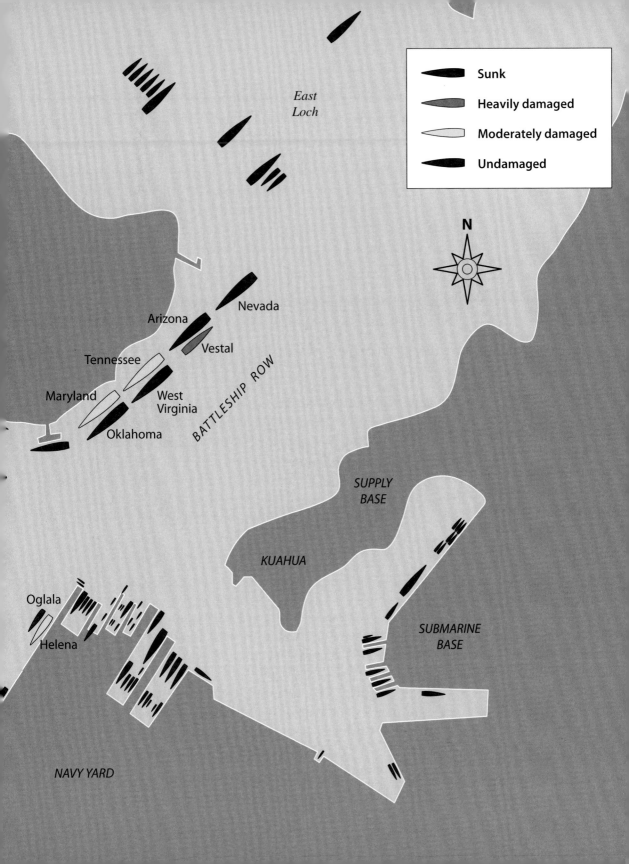

East
Loch

Sunk

Heavily damaged

Moderately damaged

Undamaged

N

Nevada

Arizona

Vestal

Tennessee

West
Virginia

Maryland

Oklahoma

BATTLESHIP ROW

SUPPLY
BASE

KUAHUA

Oglala

Helena

SUBMARINE
BASE

NAVY YARD

an attack was imminent. Military signalmen, however, could not raise Pearl Harbor on military channels, so the message was sent by slower commercial cable. By the time it arrived, Japanese planes were in the air over Pearl Harbor.

Given this flood of intelligence, historians and military analysts question why the military failed to take steps to defend Pearl Harbor. One answer might lie in the flood of messages intercepted. Few of the hundreds of intercepted diplomatic messages specifically mentioned Pearl Harbor. Those that did—requests for information on fleet deployment at Pearl, for example—were part of general requests for similar information about numerous American bases in the Pacific. While events proved that Pearl Harbor was Japan's intended target, that seemed less apparent in 1941, when bits of unconnected intelligence arrived on the president's desk on a daily basis and no one was charged with the responsibility of "connecting the dots." Ironically, the only American official who had clear intelligence regarding Pearl Harbor was FBI director J. Edgar Hoover. The information, though, was provided by a Yugoslav double agent named Dusko Popov, who had received clear indications of Japanese intentions while operating in Germany. Hoover, though, hated Slavs, despised Popov, cut his interview with Popov short, and failed to send Popov's vital information on to the president.

Although evidence is lacking or conflicting, some revisionist historians have presented scenarios that may explain U.S. failures to protect the fleet. Some of these scenarios involve a deliberate disregard for intelligence by U.S. and British leaders on the grounds that the attack would likely force America's entrance into WWII. Most historians, however, dismiss these theories as either inconsistent with the greater body of evidence, or simply convoluted and needlessly complex explanations of normal intelligence and communications failures.

Japan Weighs Its Options in Pursuing War in the Pacific

Giichi Nakahara

While open war between Japan and the United States did not begin until the attack on Pearl Harbor in December 1941, tensions between the two countries had been escalating over the course of the previous year. Much of the hostility between the two nations was based on U.S. support for China, which Japan invaded in 1937. In addition, the Japanese were apprehensive about the U.S. strengthening its alliances with both England and the Soviet Union, who were fighting Germany, Japan's political ally. Rear Admiral Giichi Nakahara, the chief of the Japanese Navy Ministry's personnel bureau, chronicled these concerns in the extracts from his diary comprised in the following viewpoint. Nakahara makes note of important events in U.S. international relations and considers the effect of these incidents on Japanese security and foreign policy. As December 7, 1941,

SOURCE. Giichi Nakahara, *The Pearl Harbor Papers*. Dulles, VA: Brassey's, 2000. Copyright © 1993 by Prange Enterprises, Inc. Reproduced by permission of Potomac Books, Inc. (formerly Brassey's Inc.).

approaches, his entries confirm the deterioration of diplomatic relations between Japan and the United States and the inevitability of war between the two countries.

11 *August 1941.* Since the Japanese occupation of Thailand [in early 1941], the hostile attitude of the U.S. and England against Japan has become very outstanding. . . .

The Russo-German war [the eastern front of World War II] seemed at a deadlock for a little time, but lately Germany is announcing considerable war results. . . .

25 Divisions out of 40 were destroyed at the battle between Kiev and Odessa [both in Russia].

At the same time, a considerable number of British ships were sunk off the British coast.

I cannot but feel that those announcements of war results by Germany is to reveal the fact that Germany wants to show that the Eastern front is not stagnantly defensive facing the severe winter soon to come, although the German attack on the USSR [the Soviet Union] was not through yet.

On the other hand, the British Empire wants positive help from the U.S. Some say that the former intends to take over Norway.

Germany is asking French help and pro-German people in France are increasing.

Rumor is running that Germany asked France to put Tagare into one of the common defense areas against England.

> Japan, too, is being forced to fight it out to the last on the Pacific; now it is high time to decide on war or peace by external pressure.

Or it might imply that the preceding paragraph is just a pretext for the U.S. to occupy it.

There is another information telling me that the U.S. is insisting on the claim to Brazil to let Brazil ask Portugal to request common defense of the Azores [Portuguese islands about 1,500 kilometers (930 miles) west of Lisbon, Portugal's capital] areas.

Japan, too, is being forced to fight it out to the last on the Pacific; now it is high time to decide on war or peace by external pressure. . . .

The U.S. Alliance with Great Britain and Russia Grows Stronger

22 August 1941. Germany has just finished the occupation of the areas west of the Nedoniapro River, captured many ships at the Nikolaiefski Naval Port; Odessa is

---

Flying the Hump: Keeping the Door to China Open

American officials in 1941 saw a vital need to keep China in World War II, yet Japan's early conquests had cut off all land routes to China. Only one air route, a very dangerous flight from airfields in eastern Assam across the High Himalayas to K'unming in China's Yunnan province, remained open. The five-hundred-mile route posed several dangers for planes of the period. It required flying at very high altitudes, adding to the dangers of violent turbulence and severe icing the dangers of enemy aircraft and frequent monsoons, which pilots encountered at any altitude. Yet, through nearly three years of war, the U.S. Army Air Forces Air Transport Command used this route as the sole means for transporting supplies and passengers to China. Begun in 1942, the airlift delivered a total of 650,000 tons, with a monthly maximum of 71,042 tons reached in July 1945. The Hump was the proving ground of [a] massive strategic airlift, demonstrating that large amounts of material could be delivered by air and presaging the Berlin Airlift of 1948–49 and emergency deliveries to Korea in 1950.

SOURCE. *Warner Stark, "Flying the Hump," Dictionary of American History. Ed. Stanley I. Kutler. 3rd ed. Vol. 3. New York: Charles Scribner's Sons, 2003.*

going to fall. At the same time, Germany has begun to take the offensive in Northern Russia.

Since the interview between the leaders of the U.S. and England on the Atlantic Ocean, the atmosphere is growing to result in the alliance of England, the United States, and Russia. Talks will be held in Moscow at the beginning of September.

The U.S. is carrying on a propaganda actively that she is supporting Russia by supplying the latter with gasoline. Rumors run that oil tankers are headed for Vladivostok. But I wonder if it is true or not.

Another rumor says that they were sent forward to the Persian Gulf.

England and Russia are putting strong pressure upon Iran. But the Shah of Iran will not respond to this.

RUSSO-JAPANESE RELATIONS: Japan will observe neutrality so long as Russia will not threaten Japan. Japan's interest in Sakhalin. Giving up helping Chiang Kai-Shek [the leader of China]. An answer from the USSR to Japan seems professedly to be quite satisfactory to us. Our reinforcement of our armed forces in Manchuria [China] does not mean any step against Russia. Concerning this Russia is very understanding, but the question is the Tripartite Agreement [the agreement signed by Germany, Italy, and Japan on September 27, 1940, establishing the alliance between the Axis powers]. . . .

THE U.S. SUPPORTS RUSSIA: It would be better for us to warn the U.S. that the American support of Russia is quite troublesome. Our information Bureau had better be silent.

THAILAND: Since the Japanese occupation of Thailand, Germany is in a different position that has been caused by the relations between Japan, England and the U.S.

It will not be long before Thailand cannot maintain friendship with Japan. The promises that have been made between the two countries will be abandoned by degrees. The Thailand Cabinet is going to be pro-England. . . .

Tensions Between the U.S. and Germany Increase

13 September 1941. During this week Leningrad [in the Soviet Union] was completely besieged by German troops and its fall has come to be a question of time.

During this week two American ships were sunk and one U.S. destroyer was attacked by a German submarine; until this time the U.S. has been very calm, but these events have made the President of the United States issue an order to attack German naval ships and airplanes in the patrol area of the U.S.

> People say that the only alternative left for us is to choose war, now that the situation stands thus, and adds that irresoluteness—neither war nor peace—cannot be borne any longer.

Germany has declared it will attack American ships to be found in the German blockaded district.

And then both countries came to show fighting conditions in special zones.

Japan will remain aloof in regard to the declaration of the United States: Lord only know! . . .

17 September 1941. Sinkings of U.S. ships have made the U.S. declare it will attack any ship of any country of the Axis that should be found in the U.S. patrol zones, whether it be a sub or an airplane; hereby the United States and Germany have entered into war substantially. . . .

The Need to Secure Nationalistic Support Within Japan

2 October 1941. The Moscow talks came to an end, according to which England and the United States will entirely cooperate with each other in aiding the Soviet by sending materials. In that talk Soviet Russia asked England to land on the western coast of Europe, but it was denounced by the British. . . .

INTERNAL SITUATION OF JAPAN: People say that the only alternative left for us is to choose war, now that the situation stands thus, and adds that irresoluteness—neither war nor peace—cannot be borne any longer. But, on the other hand, those who have property and assets are likely to stick to life. As the nation has not gone through a severe ordeal since its establishment, it is very difficult to hope that they will devote themselves to unselfish service to their mother country, service to the public good or service to one's job. . . .

11 October 1941

COMMANDER IN CHIEF OF THE COMBINED FLEET: The Fleet is now under training aiming at 8 Dec.

Although it is to be hoped that the situation would be improving in peace, yet he is quite ready for the worst case. So he need not come up to Tokyo in case the worst turns out. The order to go forward is the order to push forth to the enemy. The most important is this: in relation to the diplomatic situation, the high time to rise in war is one of the most difficult to decide—one may be too late in taking the initiative and the other may be too early. This has a close relationship with the war preparations. In regard to operational affairs and other matters concerning operational preparation, liaison should be kept more closely. . . .

15 October 1941. The German forces are around the city about 96 kilometers from Moscow, and their shells can reach the outside dispositions of the city.

The Japanese Cabinet reached the final point last night. Now we have to choose between war or peace (compromise). But the present Cabinet has no power to take the policy of war or compromise with the U.S.

If Japan should compromise with the United States, the latter would put more and more pressure over the former to the point of the former's surrender. If Japan

New York's Times Square news zipper announces Japanese actions shortly after the military raid on Pearl Harbor. (AP Images.)

should surrender to the U.S., the result would be the destruction of the Japanese race spirit. Turning the eye to the Navy, the Navy would be deemed weak and the result would be the loss of the Navy's credit among the people; then it should not even be dreamed to replete the Navy. On the contrary, the Army will turn their course to the Chinese continent with the expression of triumph on their faces as if to say "it is only the Army that can support the fatherland." But in case the policy of the Army should fail, Chiang Kai-shek or even Wang Ching-wei [leader of the Republic of China, a Japanese puppet state established in March 1940] may change sides. There will be a more difficult situation. It is now the turning point to turn the nation's eyes to the importance of the ocean from that of the Continent. If we cannot do this, we have to face the decline and fall of the mother country at last. How critical it is now! Its main cause is the deficiency of the people's understanding of the ocean. At the moment when people are going to be wakened up, all is going to be pushed back. What does this mean? . . .

26 October 1941. The United States Navy Department made a showdown that the transportation route of sending material for the aid of the Soviet was changed to Boston-Archangel course.

Of course, this is the policy of giving offense to Japan as well as to deter Japan's good start together with the freezing of funds in the U.S. Notwithstanding, this will cause a tendency among the Japanese, giving them a sort of optimistic prospect of improving diplomatic relations between the U.S. and Japan, consequently it is feared Japanese resolution may be weakened by such an opinion.

> The United States does not recognize the independence of Japan; now it is high time for Japan to decide with resolution.

The United States prefers to choose a chronic way of entering into war; the bill of arming merchant marine ships passed the Lower House, and the bill permitting passage into the blockaded area.

In England, on the other hand, there are two elements disputing each other; one is that the British forces should land on the Continent, and the other is to send needed materials to the Soviet Union, for the British Empire is not so strong as to be able to land on the Continent. Anyway, England is still agonizing how to help the USSR in this Russian crisis. Russia has promoted to use the forces in the Asiatic Far East. The crisis is so pressing. . . .

Diplomacy with the U.S. Fails

1 December 1941

MEETING OF THE CHIEFS OF BUREAUS AND DEPART-MENTS: The point of the American answer.

1. Respect for the Nine-Power Treaty in Asia [which established China's sovereignty].
2. Evacuation of Japanese armed forces from China and French Indo-China (includes Manchuria).
3. Open Door principle of the Chinese Continent, equality of trade and commerce.
4. Trade and commerce under barter system.
5. Parting from the Axis Party.

   Etc.

Eight articles in all; but, in short, it is not unthinkable to dispose of the China Incident [the name used in Japan to refer to the Sino-Japanese War since no official declaration of war was ever made] and to establish the Greater Far Asiatic Co-Prosperity Sphere [a concept propagated by Japan in which the Asian countries would be free of influence from the Western powers], and that the United States does not recognize the independence of Japan; now it is high time for Japan to decide with resolution.

The Imperial Council—decision.

Professedly, we go with two principles.

4 December 1941. Commander in Chief Admiral Yamamoto [the naval officer who led the Pearl Harbor attacks] sailed out for expedition. . . .

The Attack on Pearl Harbor Succeeds

14 December 1941. On the strength of our success at Pearl Harbor we should occupy Hawaii now, some people say. It goes without saying that it is the best policy to take Hawaii to decide the future of the Pacific. If we lose a day in occupying the Islands, our operation to capture them will be so much the more difficult. Our experience at Wake Island shows this.

However, if we fail in this, the tables will be turned favorable to the United States again in a minute. So it cannot be done so hastily. . . .

3 January 1942. Our submarines bombarded Hilo (Hawaiian Islands) and Maui and Kauai Islands. Woodpecker strategy! Will not this strategy decoy out the enemy?

Our subs chased a U.S. carrier (1) and a cruiser (1) that were coming out of the harbor, but, to our regret, they missed them.

The U.S. has to atone for the failure at Pearl Harbor, and at the same time, the morale in the U.S. Navy had to be maintained and heightened. They have to do both. By what means? Will they attack Wake, the Marshalls, Hokkaido, or Tokyo? They will not come out as far as Tokyo.

The President Asks Congress to Declare War Against Japan

Franklin D. Roosevelt

On December 8, 1941, President Franklin D. Roosevelt stood before a joint session of Congress to ask for a declaration of war against Japan in response to the attack on Pearl Harbor and other U.S. installations in the Pacific. His speech is presented in the following viewpoint. Characterizing the attacks as "dastardly" and "unprovoked," the president assures Congress—and the nation at large—that the United States has the determination and force of arms to triumph over such treacherous foes. Roosevelt, the thirty-second president of the United States, had previously steered the country through the Great Depression and would guide the U.S. through the bulk of the war years to make good on his assurance of ultimate victory.

SOURCE. Franklin D. Roosevelt, "Address of the President of the United States," Declarations of a State of War with Japan, Germany, and Italy: U.S. Senate, 77th Congress, 1st Session, Document No. 148, 1941.

Yesterday, December 7, 1941—a date which will live in infamy—the United States of America was suddenly and deliberately attacked by naval and air forces of the Empire of Japan.

The United States was at peace with that nation and, at the solicitation of Japan, was still in conversation with its Government and its Emperor looking toward the maintenance of peace in the Pacific. Indeed, 1 hour after Japanese air squadrons had commenced bombing in Oahu, the Japanese Ambassador to the United States and his colleague delivered to the Secretary of State a formal reply to a recent American message. While this reply stated that it seemed useless to continue the existing diplomatic negotiations, it contained no threat or hint of war or armed attack.

A Filipina woman lies dead after a Japanese attack on Manila. U.S. president Franklin D. Roosevelt used Japan's aggressions throughout the Pacific to convince the United States to enter World War II against Japan. (Time Life Pictures/Getty Images.)

It will be recorded that the distance of Hawaii from Japan makes it obvious that the attack was deliberately planned many days or even weeks ago. During the intervening time the Japanese Government has deliberately sought to deceive the United States by false statements and expressions of hope for continued peace.

British Prime Minister Winston Churchill Conjectures About Japan's Motives for War

Many people have been astonished that Japan should in a single day have plunged into war against the United States and the British Empire. We all wonder why, if this dark design, with all its laborious and intricate preparations, had been so long filling their secret minds, they did not choose our moment of weakness eighteen months ago. Viewed quite dispassionately, in spite of the losses we have suffered and the further punishment we shall have to take, it certainly appears to be an irrational act. It is, of course, only prudent to assume that they have made very careful calculations and think they see their way through. Nevertheless, there may be another explanation. We know that for many years past the policy of Japan has been dominated by secret societies of subalterns and junior officers of the Army and Navy, who have enforced their will upon successive Japanese Cabinets and Parliaments by the assassination of any Japanese statesman who opposed, or who did not sufficiently further, their aggressive policy. It may be that these societies, dazzled and dizzy with their own schemes of aggression and the prospect of early victories, have forced their country against its better judgment into war. They have certainly embarked upon a very considerable undertaking. For after the outrages they have committed upon us at Pearl Harbour, in the Pacific Islands, in the Philippines, in Malaya, and in the Dutch East Indies, they must now know that the stakes for which they have decided to play are mortal.

SOURCE. *Winston Churchill, address to joint session of U.S. Congress, December 26, 1941.*

Attacks All over the Pacific

The attack yesterday on the Hawaiian Islands has caused severe damage to American naval and military forces. Very many American lives have been lost. In addition American ships have been reported torpedoed on the high seas between San Francisco and Honolulu.

Yesterday the Japanese Government also launched an attack against Malaya.

Last night Japanese forces attacked Hong Kong.

Last night Japanese forces attacked Guam.

Last night Japanese forces attacked the Philippine Islands.

Last night the Japanese attacked Wake Island.

This morning the Japanese attacked Midway Island.

Japan has, therefore, undertaken a surprise offensive extending throughout the Pacific area. The facts of yesterday speak for themselves. The people of the United States have already formed their opinions and well understand the implications to the very life and safety of our Nation.

> No matter how long it may take us to overcome this premeditated invasion, the American people, in their righteous might, will win through to absolute victory.

America Will Prevail

As Commander in Chief of the Army and Navy, I have directed that all measures be taken for our defense.

Always will we remember the character of the onslaught against us.

No matter how long it may take us to overcome this premeditated invasion, the American people, in their righteous might, will win through to absolute victory.

I believe I interpret the will of the Congress and of the people when I assert that we will not only defend ourselves to the uttermost but will make very certain that this form of treachery shall never endanger us again.

Hostilities exist. There is no blinking at the fact that our people, our territory, and our interests are in grave danger.

With confidence in our armed forces with the unbounded determination of our people we will gain the inevitable triumph so help us God.

I ask that the Congress declare that since the unprovoked and dastardly attack by Japan on Sunday, December 7, a state of war has existed between the United States and the Japanese Empire.

U.S. Citizens React to the Attack on Pearl Harbor and Their Country's Entry into the War

Interviews by Paul Martin

In the days following the attack on Pearl Harbor, many Americans wrestled with feelings of surprise and anger. In this viewpoint, American journalist Paul Martin interviews first a group of Bloomington, Indiana, college students and then a subsection of the town's population to assess the reaction of typical citizens to the Japanese raid. Their responses show solidarity and a willingness to fight; however, their opinions are not homogeneous and reflect instead a broad range of feelings about what could have been done prior to the attack and what should be done to avenge the loss. This set of interviews is part of the "Man-on-the-Street" interviews coordinated by American folklorist and ethnomusicologist Alan Lomax and housed as part of the Library of Congress's Digital Library Program.

SOURCE. *After the Day of Infamy: "Man-on-the-Street" Interviews Following the Attack on Pearl Harbor,* December 10, 1941. The Library of Congress.

aul Martin: This is Wednesday, December 10, 1941. Last Sunday, three days ago, on December 7, the United States of America was attacked by armed forces of the Japanese Empire. Indiana University, in cooperation with the Library of Congress of the United States, has arranged to record some of the opinions of five representative students concerning the war at this point. These students, we believe, have opinions which should be taken into consideration because they are the people who will be bearing the brunt of this war after the war actually gets underway.

Students' First Impressions of the Attack on Pearl Harbor

First, I have upon my right, Mr. Mike Fox, a sophomore. Mr. Fox, tell us just nearly as you can just what you thought of the war when you heard of the declaration of war by Japan? I mean the attack of the Japanese planes upon Pearl Harbor last Sunday?

Mike Fox: Well, I was stunned and at first I didn't believe it.

Paul Martin: Did not believe it at first. Well, after that period left you, then what did you think about it?

Mike Fox: Oh, I'd say it was one a feeling of fury and anger that we had been betrayed.

Paul Martin: That we had been betrayed by the people who negotiated in Washington at the time of the actual attack did take place.

Mike Fox: Yes.

Mr. Boyer: I think our secretary of state must have been asleep if we were betrayed. Clearly, we need somebody in the Naval Intelligence Corps to kind of find out what's going on. If we didn't know what was going on prior to the attacks.

Paul Martin: I see. Mr. Royer believes—

Mr. Boyer: Boyer.

[*Paul Martin*]:—Mr. Boyer believes that we were asleep. Ms. Fargo?

Ms. Fargo: And yet, don't you feel at the same time that perhaps it wasn't a matter of their being asleep, but rather of holding out to the very end and maintaining an American policy which we have attempted to follow?

Male Student: I agree with Ms. Fargo very much. We weren't asleep. After all the Japanese asked for two extra weeks in negotiations. Believing this to be in the guise of friendship we did so. They even sent another ambassador, Mr. Kurusu, to interview the secretary of state. And after all under this guise, I don't think we can say anything but treachery. . . .

> We weren't asleep. After all the Japanese asked for two extra weeks in negotiations.

Ms. Fargo: Paul, . . . I wonder, getting back to your first question, if any of the rest of you felt that Germany, as a first reaction, was behind this as a very well thought out, well-timed plan? Rather than Japan itself taking a lead on this?

Paul Martin: Ms. Fossil, what was your opinion about that?

Ms. Fossil: Well, of course it was a shock. We just got in from a hike Sunday afternoon. Along came these headlines that war had been declared on the United States by Japan. I got sort of confused and told a Jewish dialect story to a bunch of Jewish students [*laughter*]. Then we thought things over a while, but it just didn't seem right that Japan should be the ones making attack. I would have expected an attack on the Atlantic, first.

The Desire to Avoid Entry into War

Paul Martin: Well, now since we have some of the attitudes which some of you hadn't at the time when you heard of the attack by Japan, I'd like to get just what some of your attitudes were concerning our foreign policy before this bombing. In other words, whether or not your attitudes were drastically changed by this bombing. Mr. Fox?

Mike Fox: Well, I was definitely a cooperationist before this. I don't believe in isolation, and never have.

Paul Martin: Cooperationist? Would you tell us what a cooperationist—

Mike Fox: Well, I believe that we should work in concert with the other democratic nations of the world. Long I have felt that the difficulty of the United States has been that we, after framing the idea of the League of Nations [the intergovernmental organization established with the Treaty of Versailles and the precursor to the United Nations, founded to prevent war], dropped out of it. Since the war broke out in 1939, I have felt that we should give England and later Russia every assistance short of war. Now, my feelings are exactly the same now that we're in it.

Mr. Boyer: I think Mr. Fox has been reading too many newspapers [*laughter*]. Of course, that is the traditional attitude. The democratic nations of the world, which there aren't any democratic nations outside of the United States, and the . . . we have cooperated economically, but we are keeping the other countries of the world on, I can't express what I mean to say. Let someone else take over.

Ms. Fargo: . . . From a student's standpoint I wonder if we don't lean a little bit towards this. Especially when we heard the president's speech the other day and heard this unanimous enthusiastic reaction from our Congressmen. We've been brought up for the past nineteen and twenty years to abhor war and to treat it as something that is not a part of our culture. And then in the past few years, I don't believe we are too surprised at the Japanese action, because we've seen what they've done in the past and we've watched them fairly closely. But, weren't we a little bit used to the idea that we wanted to avoid everything at all costs and then this sudden foreign war policy thrown upon us was rather a shock to this generation, because I for one was rather surprised at the Congressmen the other day cheering so enthusiastically. And yet, I think if I were there, I'd probably would have done the same thing.

Mr. Russell: Yes, the other idea, I think, has been instilled into the minds of the youth of this country ever since the World War that war is the greatest of all evils.

Time to Abandon Isolationist Ideologies

Paul Martin: Mr. Fox, getting back to what you said just a moment ago, you said that you believed in helping Great Britain and the other democracies win this war by every means short of war. In other words, you do not feel that the United States is at war with Germany at the present time to the same extent to which she is with Japan?

Mike Fox: I would say morally yes, but looking at the problem realistically and practically, I believe that as a military standpoint it is far better to fight on one front than on two. By concentrating our efforts on Japan, I am of the opinion that we can knock her out of the war much more rapidly than we can if our efforts [are] split by an AEF [American Expiditional Force], for example, in Africa and an Atlantic fleet which must see action in the Atlantic.

Mr. Russell: Don't forget that's just exactly what Hitler wants us to do. If we concentrate entirely upon Japan, then we must stop our flow of goods to Great Britain and

Russia. And evidently, the grand strategy pact of the Axis powers is to divert our flow of materials.

Ms. Fossil: But according to what the president said in his speech last night, he is intending to continue our shipments to Russia and to England.

Mr. Boyer: I'd like to call to Ms. Fossil's attention the fact that the only road left to Russia is now the road through Persia. And there's a lot of stock [that] lies behind the Japanese archipelago. Therefore, I believe that we can help Russia by sending all these supplies to Persia. But if we do get into the war with Germany it means splitting our resources. And just as Germany did not want to fight on more than one front, neither should we.

Ms. Fossil: In regard to that, we don't even know Russia's stand yet.

Mr. Boyer: Yes, in Germany, Germany is the base for the whole thing. I think that we should get at the base of this thing instead of going around the fringes and taking the longest way in, just go to the base and wipe that out and then the whole thing will be solved.

> I think we've gone too much on tradition now and that's the reason this Pearl Harbor incident has come out.

Paul Martin: Then you would favor an immediate declaration of war—

Mr. Boyer: That's right.

Paul Martin:—against Germany?

Mr. Boyer: That's right.

Ms. Fargo: Well, it hasn't been our policy in the past to do that.

Mr. Boyer: Well, I think we've gone too much on tradition now and that's the reason this Pearl Harbor incident has come out. We have thought of this non-combatant tradition of the United States and I think we should quit fooling around with ideologies and get down to actual fighting and what is really happening here in the world. . . .

The Attack on Pearl Harbor Arouses an American Fighting Spirit

Paul Martin: This is Wednesday, December 10, 1941. Last Sunday, December 7, the United States of America was attacked by armed forces of the Japanese Empire. The Radio Department of Indiana University, in cooperation with the Library of Congress of the United States, has arranged to record some of the opinions of four people concerning the war at this point. They believe that these four people represent a well-balanced cross-section of the citizenry at our disposal.

First, Mr. Merritt A. Calvert, a merchant. Mr. Calvert, could you tell us just as nearly as possible, what your immediate mental reaction was when hearing of the bombing of Pearl Harbor?

Merritt A. Calvert: Well, Mr. Martin it seemed here in the Middle West, that we couldn't quite realize the . . . the greatness of this project that the Japs had started. We all felt that there was maybe propaganda, newspaper talk. After all, when we heard of the bombing, the reaction we can hardly express. Everyone in this locality and around the university with as many young people as we have, was first depressed and then disgusted and now it seems that we are ready to do anything that is necessary to stop this Japanese invasion.

Paul Martin: And the shock and the horror of the first hearing of the bombing has now settled into a resolve to actually win the war no matter what we have to do. . . .

Merrit A. Calvert: That's right.

Paul Martin: Well, . . . what had been your attitude concerning the foreign policy of the United States toward Japan and toward the rest of the world before this bombing?

Merritt A. Calvert: I'm quite sure that I was just an isolationist, I—

Paul Martin: You were an isolationist?

Merritt A. Calvert: I seemed, that I should feel that we keep out of it as much as possible. But after an attack on American property, right away I am of a different opinion. . . .

> " My immediate reaction was that the attack had been framed by representatives of government wishing to draw us into the war. "

A Cowardly Attack That Could Have Been Avoided

Paul Martin: Next, is Mr. Donald E. Bowin, a lawyer. Mr. Bowin, you've heard some of the questions which I have asked Mr. Calvert. And first of all, we would like to know just what your reaction was, immediate reaction, upon hearing of the bombing of Pearl Harbor last Sunday.

Donald E. Bowin: My immediate reaction was that the attack had been framed by representatives of government wishing to draw us into the war. After I learned the true facts I did have considerable resentment for the more or less treacherous attack of the Japanese which was not only yellow, but a hit and run attack. And I now have the feeling that immediate action should be taken on the part of this government to see that the Japanese are tracked down and immediate action taken and not too much delay as has existed in the case of England's attitude in the European war.

Paul Martin: Well, yes, I think that the attack was decidedly yellow, no doubt about that. Mr. Bowin, just what was your opinion toward our foreign policy before the war began?

Donald E. Bowin: I felt that the foreign policy of the United States had been more or less a vacillating one. That we had attempted to negotiate and delay at the same time that our governmental leaders were making verbal attacks on the foreign governments. I feel that either that . . . I feel that a policy of appeasement is not the proper policy. I think that this present war in the Orient might have been avoided if the policy of appeasement had been avoided at the time that Japan seized Manchukuo.

And also, I would reference to the Munich meeting that should have been avoided. I think that the attitude as expressed by Wendell Wilkie [a lawyer with aspirations for the presidency], as an American leader, represents the true position for this country to take. I think that Wilkie was more positive in his foreign policy than President Roosevelt and I think that this nation with that type of foreign policy would not have suffered the surprise attack at Pearl Harbor. . . .

The U.S. Navy Should Have Been Patrolling the Pacific

Paul Martin: And now, Mr. Burt Laws, an electrical technician. Mr. Laws, would you tell us now as nearly as you can just what your reaction was upon immediately hearing of the bombing of Pearl Harbor last Sunday.

Burt Laws: My immediate reaction was that the radio reports were somewhat confused. I thought the bombing could have taken place in the Philippine Islands, but I was very much surprised to know that the Japanese were so versatile as to scatter their forces over the entire Pacific Ocean and reach the Hawaiian Islands.

My first thought was, where were the battleships of the American Navy that we'd been taught for so many years that were covering, scouring the Pacific Ocean and various other oceans for our immediate protection? Where were they? And according to reports, most of them were in Pearl Harbor. And my first thought was, why were they there? Why weren't they patrolling the Pacific as we'd all been taught that they more or less did most of the time.

Paul Martin: Yes, it's true that we were caught by surprise. Now, in regard to that, do you think that the policy which the United States government followed in that respect, that is of maintaining peaceful negotiations with Japan up to the very last moment. Do you believe that that policy was a good one or that we knowing that war probably was inevitable should have tried to get in the first blow?

> I think we were right in waiting until we had done everything that was possible in a diplomatic way.

Burt Laws: It has been a policy that the United States has always followed in the past I think, and diplomatic relations have always been ones that had been carried out first. And we were in that process at the time we were attacked and that more or less I guess is the reason for some of our ships being holed up in the Pearl Harbor and for us not knowing that the Japanese were scattered over the parts of the Pacific Ocean.

Diplomacy Should Be Pursued to the Last

Paul Martin: And you feel that the—well, the loss which accrued to the United States for our lateness in getting into this actual fighting war was more than made up by the feeling which the American people have because they knew that they did exhaust every effort in order to achieve peace—

Burt Laws: I think that's true. I think that is quite true.

Paul Martin: I see. What do you think about that Mr. Calvert?

Merritt A. Calvert: I think that we were right in waiting until we had done everything that was possible in a diplomatic way. There is a possibility that we waited a few hours too long. I think that in Washington, possibly somebody knew that there was no chance for settlement of our differences. And word could surely have been sent to our outposts at least, to have them on the alert for any action that we might expect from Japan knowing their history in the past as being rather sneaky with their activities in war. We could have been on the lookout for it.

Paul Martin: Mr. Bowin, what do you think about that?

Donald E. Bowin: I feel that the . . . our governmental leaders were sincere in the hope that some peace in the Pacific might be preserved. However, in view of the developments of the last few days, it would seem that at least the military authorities of our country had knowledge of the actual conditions, or should have had knowledge, of the actual conditions prior to the time of the attack on Pearl Harbor. And the attack would not have been as disastrous as it would have been if our forces had been as alert as they should have been at that time.

The U.S. Government Interns People of Japanese Descent

Western Defense Command, U.S. Army

In the aftermath of the bombing of Pearl Harbor, the U.S. government feared that some Japanese immigrants and Japanese Americans might carry out sabotage along the West Coast in the name of aiding their ancestral homeland. Because the coastal and even inland areas of Washington, Oregon, and California were home to more than 100,000 people of Japanese heritage, the government acted quickly to deal with potential fifth-column activities. President Franklin D. Roosevelt wrote several proclamations for dealing with enemy aliens, and in February 1942 he issued Executive Order 9066, which gave the military the power to evict the vast majority of Japanese and Japanese American residents from areas close to resources and installations deemed strategically important to the war effort. Most of

SOURCE. *Final Report: Japanese Evacuation from the West Coast, 1942*, Headquarters Western Defense Command and Fourth Army, Office of the Commanding General, Presidio of San Francisco, California. Washington, DC: Government Printing Office, 1943.

the evicted were sent to relocation camps in eastern California, as well as in Utah, Wyoming, Arizona, Idaho, Colorado, and Arkansas. The following viewpoint is the final report to the U.S. Army chief of staff from the commanding general of the Western Defense Command. It summarizes the rationale for relocating people of Japanese descent to protect national security. It states that it seemed more than coincidence that Japanese Americans lived near strategic shorelines, ports, and industries and that many pro-Japanese organizations among this ethnic population openly endorsed and aided Japan's cause.

On December 7 and 8th, 1941, the President [Franklin D. Roosevelt] issued proclamations declaring all nationals and subjects of the nations with which we were at war to be enemy aliens. This followed the precedent of the last war, and was based upon the same statutory enactment which supported the proclamations of President [Woodrow] Wilson in this regard. (See 50 U.S.C. 21.) By executive action, certain restrictive measures were applied against all enemy aliens on an equal basis. In continental United States, the Attorney General, through the Department of Justice, was charged with the enforcement and administration of these proclamations. Where necessary fully to implement his action, the Attorney General was assigned to responsibility of issuing administrative regulations. He was also give the authority to declare prohibited zones, to which enemy aliens were denied admittance or from which they were to be excluded in any case where the national security required. The possession of certain articles was declared by the proclamations to be unlawful, and these articles are described as contraband. Authority was granted for the internment of such enemy aliens as might be regarded by the Attorney General as dangerous to the national security if permitted to remain at large. In continental United States internment was left in any case to the discretion of the Attorney General.

Initial Forays to Round Up Contraband

On the night of December 7th and the days that followed, certain enemy aliens were apprehended and held in detention pending the determination whether to intern, essentially, the apprehensions thus effected were based on lists of suspects previously compiled by the intelligence services, the Federal Bureau of Investigation, the Office of Naval Intelligence, and the Military Intelligence Service. During the initial stage of this action, some 2,000 persons were apprehended. Japanese aliens were included in their number.

Beyond this, little was done forcefully to implement the Presidential proclamations. No steps were taken to provide for the collection of contraband and no prohibited zones were proclaimed.

The Commanding General [John DeWitt], during the closing weeks of December, requested that the War Department induce the Department of Justice to take vigorous action along the Pacific Coast. He sought steps looking toward the enforcement of the contraband prohibitions contained in the proclamations and toward the declaration of certain prohibited zones surrounding "vital installation" along the coast. The Commanding General had become convinced that the military security of the coast required these measures.

His conclusion was in part based upon interception of unauthorized radio communications which had been identified as emanating from certain areas along the coast. Of further concern to him was the fact that for a period of several weeks following December 7th, substantially every ship leaving a West Coast port was attacked by an enemy submarine. This seemed conclusively to point to the existence of hostile ship-to-shore communication.

The Commanding General requested the War Department to send a representative, and to arrange with the Department of Justice for an officer [of] that agency to meet with him at San Francisco, in order to consider the situation "on the ground." His objective was to crystallize a program of forthright action to deal with subversive segments of the population. Preliminary to this, and primarily at the request of the Commanding General, a number of discussions had been held between War and Justice Department representatives in Washington, D.C. The Provost Marshall, Major General Allen W. Gullion, the Assistant Secretary of War, Honorable John J. McCloy, the Chief of the Enemy Alien Control Unit, Department of Justice, Mr. Edward J. Ennis, and the Chief of the Aliens Division, Office of the Provost Marshal General, participated in these meetings.

> The Commanding General urged that the Justice Department provide for spot raids in various areas to determine the presence and possession of contraband.

These conferences between War and Justice Department representatives in Washington were followed by the conference requested by the Commanding General in San Francisco. Mr. James Rowe, Jr., Assistant to the Attorney General, representative the Department of Justice. The Commanding General urged that the Justice Department provide for spot raids in various areas to determine the presence and possession of contraband; that it authorize the ready seizure of contraband [and] adopt means for collecting and storing it. He further requested that the Attorney General declare prohibited zones surrounding certain coastal installations. These conferences continued over the period between January 2nd and 5th, 1942, and, as an outgrowth of these meetings, the Department of Justice agreed to a program of enforcement substantially as desired by the Commanding General and Mr. Rowe. . . .

Establishing Prohibited Zones

After a series of surveys made by the Commanding Generals of the several Western Defense Command sectors, the Commanding General submitted a number of recommendations calling for the establishment of 99 prohibited zones in the State of California, and two restricted zones. These were to be followed by similar recommendations pertaining to Arizona, Oregon, and Washington. Primarily, the prohibited zones in Cali-

WAR RELOCATION AUTHORITY (WRA) RELOCATION CENTERS

Taken from: Jeffrey F. Burton et al. *Confinement and Ethnicity: An Overview of World War II Japanese American Relocation Sites.* Tucson: Western Archaelogical and Conservation Center, 1999.

Japanese-born Americans arrive at the Manzanar War Relocation Center. About 115,000 people of Japanese descent living on the west coast of the United States were forcibly relocated to internment camps under suspicion that they might aid the Japanese military. **(Time & Life Pictures/Getty Images.)**

fornia surrounded various points along the California Coast, installations in the San Francisco Bay area, particularly along the waterfront, and in Los Angeles and San Diego. The recommendation as to California was transmitted by the Commanding General by letter dated January 21, 1942, and was received from the Commanding General by the War Department on January 25, 1942, and was forwarded by the Secretary of War to the Attorney General on the same date.

In a series of press releases, the Attorney General designated as prohibited zones the 99 areas recommended by the Commanding General in California. Considerable evacuation thus was necessitated, but most of the enemy aliens concerned were able to take up residence

in or near places adjacent to the prohibited zone. For example, a large prohibited zone followed the San Francisco waterfront area. Enemy aliens living in this section were required only to move elsewhere in San Francisco. Of course, only aliens of enemy nationality were affected, and no persons of Japanese ancestry born in the United States were required to move under the program.

Although some problems were presented which required provision for individual assistance, essentially there was little of this involved. By arrangement with the Justice Department, the associated agencies of the Federal Security Agency were asked to lend assistance in unusually needy cases.

Mr. Tom C. Clark, then the West Coast representative of the Anti-Trust Division of the Justice Department, supervised this phase of enemy alien control and coordinated all activities for the Justice Department. There was much conjecture that this was the forerunner of a general enemy alien evacuation. Mr. Clark and his Anti-Trust Division staff were deluged with inquiries and comments. Conflicting reports and rumors were rampant along the coast; public excitement in certain areas reached a high pitch, and much confusion characterized the picture. However, in essence, there was no substantial dislocation or disruption socially or economically of the affected Groups.

Need for Military Control and for Evacuation

The Commanding General, meantime, prepared and submitted recommendations for the establishment of prohibited zones in Arizona, Oregon, and Washington, similar to those he had prepared for California. Upon receipt of these supplemental recommendations, forwarded by the Secretary of War, the Attorney General declined to act until further study. In the case of Washington State, the recommended prohibited zone included virtually all of the territory lying west of the Cascades. A general enemy alien evacuation from this area would have been required. More than 9,500 persons would have been affected. No agency was then prepared to supervise or conduct a mass movement, and the Attorney General was not convinced of the necessity.

As early as January 5, however, the Commanding General pointed to the need for careful advanced planning to provide against such economic and social dislocations as might [ensue] from any necessary mass evacuation. This was made eminently clear in a memorandum dated January 5, 1942, from the Commanding General to Mr. Rowe, during their initial conference at San Francisco. The point was also established that the Army had no wish to assume any aspects of civil control if there were any means by which the necessary security measures could be taken through normal civilian channels. . . .

> "Whether by design or accident, virtually always their communities were adjacent to very vital shore installations, war plants, etc."

The Attorney General, on February 9, 1942, formally advised the Secretary of War, by letter, that he could not accept the recommendation of the Commanding General for the establishment of a zone prohibited to enemy aliens in the States of Washington and Oregon of the extent required by him. . . .

Strategic Concentrations of Japanese Americans

When the Attorney General advised that his Department was not in a position to declare as prohibited to enemy aliens the extensive areas recommended for such action in Oregon and Washington, he did not thereby establish the need for military control. It had become apparent that even those measures would not have satisfied the military necessities facing the Commanding General.

For, by these means, no control would have been exerted over nearly two-thirds of the total Japanese population. Only about one-third were aliens subject to enemy alien regulations.

Because of the ties of race, the intense feeling of filial piety and the strong bonds of common tradition, culture and customs, this population presented a tightly-knit racial group. It included in excess of 115,000 persons deployed along the Pacific Coast. Whether by design or accident, virtually always their communities were adjacent to very vital shore installations, war plants, etc. While it is believed that some were loyal, it was known that many were not. It was impossible to establish the identity of the loyal and the disloyal with any degree of safety. It was not [that] there was insufficient time in which to make such a determination; it was simply a matter of facing the realities that a positive determination could not be made, that an exact separation of the "sheep from the goats" was unfeasible.

It could not be established, of course, that the location of thousands of Japanese adjacent to strategic points verified the existence of some vast conspiracy to which all of them were parties. Some of them doubtless resided there through mere coincidence. It seems equally beyond doubt, however, that the presence of others was not mere coincidence. It was difficult to explain the situation in Santa Barbara County, for example, by coincidence alone.

Throughout the Santa Maria Valley in that County, including the cities of Santa Maria and Guadalupe, every utility, air field, bridge, telephone and power line, or other facility of importance was flanked by Japanese. They even surrounded the oil fields in this area. Only a few miles south, however, in the Santa Ynez Valley, lay an area equally as productive agriculturally as the Santa Maria Valley and with lands equally available for purchase and lease, but without any strategic installations whatever. There were no Japanese in the Santa Ynez Valley.

Similarly, along the coastal plain of Santa Barbara County from Gaviota south, the entire plain, though narrow, had been subject to intensive cultivation. Yet, the only Japanese in this area were located immediately adjacent to such widely separated points as the El Capitan Oil Field, Elwood Oil Field, Summerland Oil Field, Santa Barbara airport, and Santa Barbara lighthouse and harbor entrance. There were no Japanese on the equally attractive lands between these points. In the north end of the county is a stretch of open beach ideally suited for landing purposes, extending for 15 or 20 miles, on which almost the only inhabitants are Japanese.

Such a distribution of the Japanese population appeared to manifest something more than coincidence. In any case, it was certainly evident that the Japanese population of the Pacific Coast was, as a whole, ideally situated with reference to points of strategic importance, to carry into execution a tremendous program of sabotage on a mass scale should any considerable number of them have been inclined to do so.

U.S. Organizations Loyal to Japan

There were other very disturbing indications that the Commanding General could not ignore. He was forced to consider the character of the Japanese colony along the coast. While this is neither the place nor the time to record in detail significant pro-Japanese activities in the United States, it is pertinent to note some of them in passing. Research has established that there were over 124 separate Japanese organizations along the Pacific Coast engaged, in varying degrees, in common pro-Japanese purposes. This number does not include local branches of parent organizations, of which there were more than 310.

Research and co-ordination of information had made possible the identification of more than 100 parent fascistic or militaristic organizations in Japan which have some relation, either direct or indirect, with Japanese organizations or individuals in the United States. Many of the former were parent organizations of subsidiary or branch organizations in the United States and in that capacity directed organizational and functional activities. There was definite information that the great majority of activities followed a line of control from the Japanese government, through key individuals or associations to the Japanese residents in the United States.

> That the Japanese associations, as organizations [with branches in America], aided the military campaigns of the Japanese Government is beyond doubt.

That the Japanese associations, as organizations, aided the military campaigns of the Japanese Government is beyond doubt. The contributions of these associations toward the Japanese war effort had been freely published in Japanese newspapers throughout California. . . .

The number of American-born Japanese who had been sent to Japan for education and who were now in the United States could not be overlooked. For more than twenty-five years American-born progeny of alien Japanese had been sent to Japan by their parents for education and indoctrination. There they remained for extended periods, following which they ordinarily returned to the United States. The extent of their influence upon other Nisei Japanese [the first generation of Japanese immigrants born outside of Japan] could not be accurately calculated. But it could not be disregarded. . . .

Evacuation from Strategic Areas

It was, perforce, a combination of factors and circumstances with which the Commanding General had to deal. Here was a relatively homogeneous, unassimilated element bearing a close relationship through ties of race, religion, language, custom, and indoctrination to the enemy.

The mission of the Commanding General was to defend the West Coast from enemy attack, both from within and without. The Japanese were concentrated along the coastal strip. The nature of this area and its relation to the national war effort had to be carefully considered.

The areas ultimately evacuated of all persons of Japanese ancestry embraced the coastal area of the Pacific slope. In the States of Washington and Oregon to the north, Military Area No. 2 [a length of land comprising the eastern half of California and parts of Washington and Oregon] contains all that portion lying westerly of the eastern bases of the Cascade Mountains. In other words, the coastal plain, the forests, and the mountain barrier. In California the evacuation program encompassed the entire State—that is to say, not only Military Area No. 1 [a huge swath of land running along the western shores of Washington, Oregon, and California and the southern border region of Arizona] but also Military Area No. 2. Military Area No. 2 in California was evacuated because (1) geographically and strategically the eastern boundary of the State of California approximates the easterly limit of Military Area No. 1 in Washington and Oregon, and because (2) the natural forests and mountain barriers, from which it was determined to exclude all Japanese, lie in Military Area No. 2 in California, although these lie in Military Area No. 1 of Washington and Oregon. A brief reference to the relationship of the coastal states to the national war effort is here pertinent.

That part of the States of Washington, Oregon, and California which lies west of the Cascade and Sierra Nevada Ranges, is dominated by many waterways, forests, and vital industrial installations. Throughout the Puget Sound area there are many military and naval establishments as well as shipyards, airplane factories, and other industries essential to total war. In the vicinity of Whidby Island, Island County, Washington, at the north end of the island, is the important Deception Pass bridge. This bridge provides the only means of transit by land from important naval installations, facilities, and properties in the vicinity of Whidby Island. This island afforded an ideal rendezvous from which enemy agents might communicate with enemy submarines in the Strait of Juan de Fuca or with other agents on the Olympic Peninsula. From Whidby and Camano Islands, comprising Island County, the passages through Admiralty Inlet, Skagit Bay, and Saratoga Passage from Juan de Fuca Strait to the vital areas of the Bremerton Navy Yard and Bainbridge Island can be watched. The important city of Seattle with its airplane plants, airports, waterfront facilities, Army and Navy transport establishments, and supply terminals required that an unassimilated group of doubtful loyalty be removed a safe distance from these critical areas. . . . [There is] a high concentration of persons of Japanese ancestry in the Puget Sound area. Seattle is the principal port in the Northwest; it is the port from which troops in Alaska are supplied; its inland water route to Alaska passes the north coast of Washington into the Straits of Georgia on its way to Alaska.

> The [western] coastline is particularly vulnerable. Distances between inhabited areas are great and enemy activities might be carried on without interference.

The lumber industry is of vital importance to the war effort. The State of Washington, with Oregon and California close seconds, produces the bulk of sawed lumber in the United States. The large area devoted to this industry afforded saboteurs unlimited freedom of action. The danger from forest fires involved not only the destruction of valuable timber but also threatened cities, towns, and other installations in the affected area. The entire coastal strip from Cape Flattery south to Lower California is particularly important from a protective viewpoint. There are numerous naval installations with such facilities constantly under augmentation. The coastline is particularly vulnerable. Distances between inhabited areas are great and enemy activities might be carried on without interference.

The petroleum industry of California and its great centers of production for aircraft and shipbuilding are a vital part of the lifeblood of a nation at war. The crippling of any part of this would seriously impede the war effort. Through the ports of Seattle, Portland, San Francisco, Los Angeles, and San Diego flow the sinews of war—the men, equipment, and supplies for carrying the battle against the enemy in the Pacific. . . . [A] high concentration of this segment of the population surround nearly all these key installations.

In his estimate of the situation, then, the Commanding General found a tightly knit, unassimilated racial group, substantial numbers of whom were engaged in pro-Japanese activities. He found them concentrated in great numbers along the Pacific Coast, an area of the utmost importance to the national war effort. These considerations were weighed against the progress of the Emperor's Imperial Japanese forces in the Pacific. . . .

In summary, the Commanding General was confronted with the Pearl Harbor experience, which involved a positive enemy knowledge of our patrols, our naval dispositions, etc., on the morning of December 7th; with the fact that ships leaving West Coast ports were being intercepted regularly by enemy submarines; and with the fact that an enemy element was in a position to do great damage and substantially to aid the enemy nation. Time was of the essence.

The Commanding General, charged as he was with the mission of providing for the defense of the West Coast, had to take into account these and other military considerations. He had no alternative but to conclude that the Japanese constituted a potentially dangerous element from the viewpoint of military security—that military necessity required their immediate evacuation to the interior. The impelling military necessity had become such that any measures other than those pursued along the Pacific Coast might have been "too little and too late."

CHAPTER 2

Controversies Surrounding the Attack on Pearl Harbor

The Roosevelt Administration Made Scapegoats of the Military Commanders in Hawaii

George Morgenstern

In the viewpoint that follows, George Morgenstern asserts that immediately after the attack on Pearl Harbor, the Franklin D. Roosevelt administration pinned the blame for the disaster on the chief U.S. military commanders in the region: Navy admiral Husband E. Kimmel and Army major general Walter Short. Morgenstern claims that both men were unjustly made into scapegoats because the administration knew that military staff in Washington were apprised of the coming conflict and failed to alert Kimmel and Short in time. According to Morgenstern, the administration pushed both men into early retirement quickly

Photo on previous page: Shortly before the bombing of Pearl Harbor, Japanese consulates in U.S. cities began burning their papers. Some contend that military commanders in Hawaii should have construed that as a sign that an attack was imminent. (**AP Images.**)

SOURCE. George Morgenstern, *Pearl Harbor: The Story of the Secret War.* New York: Devin-Adair, 1947, pp. 38–47.

before any nonpartisan investigation of alleged "dereliction of duty" charges could be mounted. Only a late-war congressional investigation brought forth witnesses that cast doubt on the blame attached to the two commanders, yet the findings of this committee did not influence the Department of Defense to retract its initial conclusions. George Morgenstern was a member of the editorial staff of the *Chicago Tribune* when he wrote *Pearl Harbor: The Story of the Secret War*, the first book to question the U.S. government's ignorance of the surprise attack.

In the excitement and confusion on December 7, 1941, it was not immediately noticed that the leaders of the [Franklin D.] Roosevelt administration were frantically scurrying about proving their surprise and injury, shouldering the blame for the disaster at Pearl Harbor away from themselves. Events were moving too fast for citizens to detect that the disengaging tactics of the politicians were far more successful than had been those of the Pacific fleet. . . .

There had been ominous reports of the losses at Pearl Harbor. The first Japanese claims were that the battleships "West Virginia" and "Oklahoma" had been sunk and that four other capital ships and four cruisers had been damaged. The first report from the American government came from the White House on December 8. About 3,000 casualties, equally divided between dead and wounded, were acknowledged by Roosevelt, while it was said that one old battleship had capsized, a destroyer had blown up, several other smaller ships had been seriously damaged, a large number of planes had been put out of commission, and several hangars destroyed in the bombing of Army and Navy air fields. . . .

The first "official" report on the damage was to come from Secretary [of the Navy, William Franklin] Knox. At 8:00 A.M., December 9, Knox left Washington in his own plane, "conscious," as [authors Forrest] Davis and [Ernest K.] Lindley put it, "of his share in the blame for the surprise attack at Pearl Harbor. . . . The Secretary of the Navy regarded his mission as an expiation."

Upon his return to Washington, December 15, Knox hurried to the White House and conferred with Roosevelt. Later he called the press to his office and announced a total of 2,897 Army and Navy dead, 879 wounded, and 26 missing. The "Arizona," "Utah," "Shaw," "Cassin," "Downes," and "Oglala," he said, had been sunk; the "Oklahoma" was capsized but salvageable, and other vessels had suffered damage requiring repairs of a week to several months.

An Immediate Decision to Relieve Kimmel and Short

Knox's published report had been prepared with the assistance of Comdr. Leland P. Lovette, whom the Secretary found at Pearl Harbor, where Lovette was commander of Destroyer Division 5, which included the "Cassin," "Downes," and "Shaw," all of which had been wrecked in the Jap attack. Lovette, subsequently to be named director of Navy public relations by Knox, was an officer-author of some reputation. The statement which he and Knox drew up for submission to the public emphasized the heroism of the men at Pearl Harbor, but carefully refrained from giving the American people anything like a true accounting of the damage suffered by the fleet.

> Although [Secretary of the Navy William] Knox in a private report to Roosevelt . . . did not impute exclusive or even specific blame to the Hawaiian commanders, Kimmel and Short were then assigned the role of scapegoats for the disaster.

More important than what Knox chose to tell the people was the decision which he and Roosevelt reached at their conference preceding the release of the report. It would not be known for another four years that, although Knox in a private report to Roosevelt at this very meeting did not impute exclusive or even specific blame to the Hawaiian commanders, [Admiral Husband E.] Kimmel and [Major General Walter] Short were then assigned the role of scapegoats for the disaster. Adm. [Harold] Stark, chief of naval operations in 1941, testified at the Congressional investigation in 1945 that the first thing Knox did after conferring with the President was to issue orders for the removal of Adm. Kimmel as commander of the Pacific fleet. Asked whether Knox's action was based on orders from Roosevelt, Stark said, "You always need the President's permission to remove a fleet commander."

At his press conference, however, Knox made no admission that any such action would be taken. "The United States services were not on the alert against a surprise attack on Hawaii," his report stated. "This fact calls for a formal investigation which will be initiated immediately by the President. Further action is, of course, dependent on the facts and recommendations made by this investigating board."

Knox sought to create the impression that any assessment of blame would await later investigation by an impartial commission. The impression he gave the press and the nation was wholly disingenuous. He and the President had already decided to put the onus on Kimmel and Short. The commanders were relieved of their posts, but the announcement was held up for two days, until December 17. Maj. Gen. Martin, commander of the Army Air Forces in Hawaii, was relieved at the same time.

Roosevelt Appoints a Commission After the Fact

On December 16, Roosevelt, moved by a rising tide of indignation in Congress which made it apparent that an investigation by that body was likely, forestalled independent inquiry by appointing his own investigating commission. This was a five-man board of inquiry headed

Who Was Blamed and Who Was Exonerated for the Disaster at Pearl Harbor

Two days after the Japanese attack, the first formal inquiry into the disaster began when Navy Secretary Frank Knox flew to Hawaii to see the damage first-hand. While noting that neither the army nor the navy had adequately prepared for a carrier-borne assault, Knox credited the disaster to superior Japanese planning rather than negligence on the part of American commanders. A second committee, chaired by Supreme Court Justice Owen Roberts, blamed Admiral Husband E. Kimmel, commander of the Pacific fleet, and General Walter C. Short, commander of the Hawaiian department, when it issued its findings in January 1942. While exonerating senior leaders, including Secretary of State Cordell Hull, Secretary of War Henry Stimson, and Army Chief of Staff George C. Marshall, the Roberts Commission concluded that Kimmel and Short received adequate warning of a possible Japanese attack but failed to act accordingly.

SOURCE. *Sidney L. Pash, "Pearl Harbor Investigation," Americans at War. Ed. John P. Resch. Vol. 3: 1901–1945. Detroit: Macmillan Reference USA, 2005.*

by Associate Justice Owen J. Roberts of the United States Supreme Court, who had been a proponent of war as a means of achieving world-government.

The other members were two retired admirals, Rear Adm. William H. Standley, former chief of naval operations, and Rear Adm. Joseph M. Reeves, former commander-in-chief of the United States fleet, Maj.

Gen. Frank R. McCoy, retired, and Joseph T. McNarney, a brigadier general on the active list of the Army Air Corps. McNarney later was promoted to the rank of four-star general, became deputy chief of staff, second only to Gen. Marshall in the Army hierarchy, and, finally, commander of all occupation forces in Europe. The selection of these men was not accidental. Reeves was the first commander-in-chief of the fleet to take it to Pearl Harbor. He was therefore disqualified from criticizing the selection of Pearl Harbor as its base. Standley, retired in 1937, was recalled to active duty March 6, 1941, and would not be disposed to criticize the decisions of the Navy leadership in Washington, of which he had formerly been a ranking member as chief of naval operations. McCoy, as president of the Foreign Policy Association, per se was a staunch supporter of Roosevelt's diplomacy. McNarney was a member of the Marshall clique which ran the War Department. Since 1939 he had been a member of the general staff, which was responsible for the failure to build up the defenses of Pearl Harbor and which withheld knowledge of Japanese designs and intentions from the field commanders.

> Roosevelt had already tried the case. Without calling witnesses, he found Kimmel and Short guilty, condemned them, and carried out his sentence.

Four of these men later were the recipients of honor and favors from the Roosevelt administration. Five and one-half years after his retirement with the rank of rear admiral, Reeves was promoted to admiral on the retired list June 16, 1942. This was five months after he had signed the Roberts report. Standley was decorated by Roosevelt with the Distinguished Service Medal after signing the report, and was appointed ambassador to Russia, a post which he held in 1942 and 1943. McCoy was appointed chairman of the Far Eastern Advisory Commission when allied control was established following the surrender of Japan. McNarney's meteoric rise in the Army has been described.

Roosevelt, in fixing jurisdiction, charged the commission with determining whether "any derelictions of duty or error of judgment on the part of United States Army or Navy personnel contributed to such successes as were achieved by the enemy" in "the attack made by Japanese forces upon the territory of Hawaii." These instructions were intended to exclude consideration of the behavior of official Washington.

Roosevelt had already tried the case. Without calling witnesses, he found Kimmel and Short guilty, condemned them, and carried out his sentence. He announced their removal from command the very day that the Roberts Commission assembled in Washington. Under the circumstances, it was hardly surprising that the President's hand-picked commission should report findings to order. On January 24 it submitted a report to Roosevelt which held that Kimmel and Short were guilty of "dereliction of duty."

The Roberts Report Ignored Many Facts

The report ignored many vital considerations and its findings on points of major importance were contradicted in both the Army and Navy reports of a later day and in testimony before the Congressional Investigating Committee. In addition, the findings of the commission were based upon misinformation and errors in fact. The minority report of the Joint Congressional Committee remarks:

> It is extremely unfortunate that the Roberts Commission report was so hasty, inconclusive, and incomplete. Some witnesses were examined under oath; others were not. Much testimony was not even recorded. The commission knew that Japanese messages had been intercepted and were available, prior to the attack, to the high command in Washington. The commission did not inquire

about what information these intercepts contained, who received them, or what was done about them, although the failure of Washington to inform the commanders in Hawaii of this vital intelligence bears directly on the question of whether those commanders performed their full duties. Mr. Justice Roberts testified before this committee: "I would not have bothered to read it [the intercepted Japanese traffic] if it had been shown to us."

If it were necessary to do so, detailed examples of the many short-comings of the Roberts Commission could be set forth. . . . It should be noted, however, that Justice Roberts had sufficient legal experience to know the proper method of collecting and preserving evidence which in this case involved the highest interests of the nation. The facts were then fresh in the minds of key witnesses in Washington. They could not then have been ignorant of their whereabouts at important times or have forgotten the details of events and operations. No files would have been "lost" and no information would have been distorted by the passage of time. The failure to observe these obvious necessities is almost as tragic to the cause of truth as the attack on Pearl Harbor itself was a tragedy for the nation.

For example, although the report did not mention that the United States had cracked the Japanese code months before Pearl Harbor, the commission had been informed by the chief of naval intelligence, Adm. [Theodore Stark] Wilkinson, that all of the information from Jap code intercepts had been sent to the Hawaiian commanders. In fact, only a few of the hundreds of these messages, and none of major importance, had been relayed to Kimmel and Short. Four years later, when he was examined by the congressional Pearl Harbor investigating committee, Wilkinson "corrected" the statements he had given the Roberts Commission.

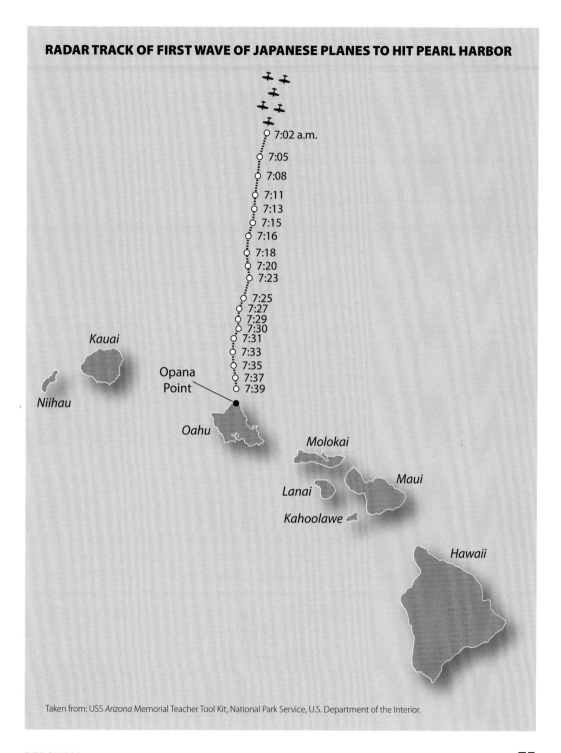

RADAR TRACK OF FIRST WAVE OF JAPANESE PLANES TO HIT PEARL HARBOR

Taken from: USS *Arizona* Memorial Teacher Tool Kit, National Park Service, U.S. Department of the Interior.

> "The [Roberts] commission greatly emphasized such information as could be construed to have given the Hawaiian commanders warning that war was imminent, but it withheld reference to the far more vital intelligence which was not transmitted to Hawaii.

Do-Don't Messages Used to Condemn the Commanders

The report held that Short's alert against sabotage "was not adequate," but had only the gentlest sort of criticism for his superiors in Washington, who had been informed by him of the action he had taken and had not even responded, let alone ordered him to go on an all-out alert. It criticized Kimmel for not taking "appropriate measures" in view of "war warnings," but held that in ordering attacks to be made upon Japanese submarines found in operating areas around Oahu, he had exceeded the authority given him by the Navy Department.

The commission greatly emphasized such information as could be construed to have given the Hawaiian commanders warning that war was imminent, but it withheld reference to the far more vital intelligence which was not transmitted to Hawaii. Of seven warning messages from Washington to Short and Kimmel which were recorded in the Roberts report, no less than four referred to the danger of sabotage. Not one suggested the possibility of surprise air attack.

These so-called warnings were so qualified by hampering instructions that the Army Board of Inquiry in its report, drafted in October, 1944, called them "do-don't" messages. The actual effect of the messages was to transfer responsibility from Washington to the field commanders if anything went wrong, but so to tie the hands of the commanders and restrict the course of action open to them that they were in no position to meet the attack when it came. The Roberts report devoted no attention to the fact that Washington had definite and detailed intelligence in the days preceding the attack that

war was coming within predictable limits of time and had ample reason to believe the Jap blow would fall on Pearl Harbor.

On December 7, Gen. [George C.] Marshall had opportunity to warn the Hawaii commanders that all evidence available to Washington indicated that an attack was coming. He sent a message, but its transmission was so botched that it reached Gen. Short seven hours

General Walter C. Short was one of two military leaders the Franklin D. Roosevelt administration blamed for the military defeat at Pearl Harbor. (Time & Life Pictures/Getty Images.)

too late. The Roberts report stated that at about 6:30 A.M., Honolulu time, Marshall dispatched "an additional warning message indicating an almost immediate break in relations between the United States and Japan." It continued, "Every effort was made to have the message reach Hawaii in the briefest possible time, but due to conditions beyond the control of any one concerned, the delivery of this urgent message was delayed until after the attack." The message, the report said, was "intended to reach both commanders in the field at about 7:00 A.M., Hawaii time," but the report adds that even "if the message had reached its destination at the time intended, it would still have been too late" because dispositions made by Kimmel and Short "were inadequate to meet a surprise air attack." By such statements, the commission glossed over Marshall's mishandling of a crucial dispatch which could have averted much of the damage suffered at Hawaii.

Diverting Blame Away from Washington

The commission, although charged with seeking derelictions of duty and errors of judgment only among Army and Navy officers, was at pains to state that Gen. Marshall, Adm. Stark, and Secretaries [Cordell] Hull [Secretary of State], [Henry L.] Stimson [Secretary of War], and Knox had discharged their responsibilities. In Conclusion 17, however, it implied that these officials did bear some responsibility, after all. It said that the dereliction of Kimmel and Short consisted of failing to "consult and confer . . . respecting the meaning and intent of the warnings" dispatched from Washington. It need hardly be said that such action would not have been necessary if the warnings were clear and precise. By a curious exercise of inverted logic, the commission also advanced the contention that because Washington was keeping them in the dark on the vital intelligence obtained from Japanese code intercepts, Kimmel and Short by some process of clairvoyance should have realized the necessity of placing a more urgent degree of readiness in effect. The report said in this connection, "Both commanders were handicapped by lack of information as to Japanese dispositions and intent. The lack of such knowledge rendered more urgent the initiation of a state of readiness for defense." Kimmel and Short did not know until much later that Washington even possessed information of the character which was being withheld from them.

> [Admiral] Kimmel, upon later inspection of the record of his own testimony [to the Roberts Commission], said that he found so many errors in the record that he spent two days correcting it.

Pushed into Retirement

Adm. Kimmel said that the Roberts Commission had informed him that he was not on trial. Kimmel, upon later inspection of the record of his own testimony, said that he found so many errors in the record that he spent two days correcting it, only to have the board refuse to change his statements as recorded originally. All that the investigators would do finally was to attach the corrected statement to the minutes. He said of the commission, "It permitted me to testify—that's all."

Gen. Short said that upon his relief from command in Hawaii he had reached Oklahoma City when he read the report of the Roberts Commission in the press. He said:

> When I read the findings of the Roberts Commission, I was dumbfounded. To be accused of dereliction of duty after almost 40 years of loyal and competent service was beyond my comprehension. I immediately called Gen. Marshall on the telephone. He was an old and trusted friend of 39 years' standing. I asked him what I should do—having the country and war in mind should I retire? He replied, "Stand pat, but if it becomes necessary I will use this conversation as authority."

Short said that, having faith in Marshall's "judgment and loyalty," he wrote Marshall a personal letter and inclosed a formal application for retirement, to be used only if Marshall thought it desirable. His covering letter was not produced in evidence before the congressional committee, but a memorandum from Marshall to Secretary Stimson on January 26, 1942, reporting Short's telephone call of the day before, stated, "I am now of the opinion that we should accept Gen. Short's application for retirement today and do this quietly, without any publicity at the moment. Adm. Stark has requested me to advise him if we do this, as he proposes to communicate this fact to Kimmel in the hope that Kimmel will likewise apply for retirement." This correspondence demonstrates that, the day after reassuring Short, Marshall took steps in secret to get rid of him.

> "The Pearl Harbor commanders were driven in disgrace from their professional careers, having been identified thoroughly in the minds of the public as bearing the sole blame for the Pearl Harbor disaster.

The War Department's order accepting Short's application for retirement was drafted after Stimson consulted Attorney General Francis J. Biddle as to how it should be worded. As finally phrased, Short's retirement was "accepted without condonation of any offense or prejudice to any future disciplinary action." The implication of this language was that Short faced court-martial action at some future date, and its effect was to seal his lips and to prevent him from making any defense of himself until he should be called for trial.

Once in possession of Short's resignation, Roosevelt, Knox, and Stimson proceeded to use it as a lever to induce Kimmel to retire. Adm. Stark notified him on orders from Secretary Knox that Short had asked to be retired. "I took this as a suggestion and I submitted a similar request," Kimmel said. "Up to that time I never considered retiring. It had not even entered my head, but I thought it over and decided that if the Navy wanted it that way, I would not stand in the way."

Kimmel thereupon forwarded a request for retirement to Washington, but two days after sending his application was informed by Stark that the notification of Gen. Short's application was not meant to influence him. Although he then modified his request for retirement by telling the Navy he wanted to do whatever would best serve the country, he received a letter from Knox on February 16 peremptorily ordering him to retire as of March 1, also "without condonation of any offense or prejudice to future disciplinary action." . . .

Thus the Pearl Harbor commanders were driven in disgrace from their professional careers, having been identified thoroughly in the minds of the public as bearing the sole blame for the Pearl Harbor disaster. The leaders of the Roosevelt administration and of its Army and Navy high command, who were in possession of the untold story of the catastrophe, saw to it that no hint of the concealed facts should leak out. Censorship and the pretext of "national security" enabled them for four years to suppress all facts which could damage them [until Congress reopened the case in 1944].

All U.S. Citizens Must Take Responsibility for the Lack of National Preparedness

Thomas E. Dewey

At a dinner given by the Economic Club of New York in January 1942, former New York district attorney Thomas E. Dewey gave a speech chastising Americans for their lack of vigilance in safeguarding the nation. The following viewpoint comprises the bulk of Dewey's speech in which he claims that it is easy to assign the blame for the surprise attack at Pearl Harbor on military leaders but more difficult for every U.S. citizen to accept the responsibility for the disaster. In Dewey's opinion, the people of the United States had become complacent in the years after World War I, and few did anything to shore up the nation's defenses in case of another conflict. Specifically, Dewey takes issue with the Roberts Report (drafted by a presidential com-

SOURCE. Thomas E. Dewey, "Our Home Front: We All Have Our Own Private Pearl Harbor," *Vital Speeches of the Day*, vol. 8, January 27, 1942, pp. 267–69. Reproduced by permission of the literary estate of the author.

mission) on the Pearl Harbor incident, suggesting that the commanders and politicians tried to hide their ineptness and their lack of action in the face of warning signs that U.S. security was compromised. He expects that every American must learn how to behave in a wartime crisis: rationing food, adjusting to shortages, overcoming selfishness, and working towards victory. In 1943, Dewey became governor of New York, a position he held for twelve years.

It is hard to believe we are in the war. Here are a thousand or thereabouts of New York's citizens in dinner clothes, eating a dinner which is unrationed, with the usual excellent food. The hotel is adequately heated; we even had sugar and they didn't tell us how many lumps we should take. It is hard to believe we are in the war, and yet, within the last two days we have had before us two sharp reminders of some of the realities which we recognize in speeches and as we read the press, but not in our thinking, or, I regret to say, in the conduct of most of the American nation.

Twenty-four years ago, yesterday, we had been in the war [World War I] 8 months and things which no one of us yet contemplate nor believe is possible, were then introduced. Wheatless bread became the order of the day and within a reasonably short time bread consisted of a small portion of wheat and a substantial portion of other cereals. We think of ourselves as the Granary of the World, with colossal wealth and grain surpluses generally, and the market being glutted with hogs and cattle. Those things are of yesterday, because we today have allies to feed who are hungry all over the globe.

It was twenty-four years ago today that the meatless Wednesdays were instituted; yet it is hard to think of the meatless Wednesdays here. And at that time heatless Mondays were instituted and lawyers and bankers and brokers were expected to live in unheated offices on Mondays.

A National Neglect of Duty

The second item of which I speak is the onslaught on Pearl Harbor. We have two ideas as a people, as regards that report. We may accept it in a common spirit; we may make two scapegoats in the matter of [U.S. Navy admiral Husband E.] Kimmel and [U.S. Army lieutenant general Walter] Short, and say, "We have found the villains in the plot"—and go about our business, and meanwhile building up ourselves a hero on the other side so that we may sleep peacefully at night and not see Japs crawling under the bed.

On the other hand we may read that report a second time, understanding the implications, and awake to what it means to all of us. We may awake to the sense of responsibility which the implications of that report bring home to every man and woman over the age of 16, shall I say—and their own personal responsibility for all of the implications of that report.

Personally, I choose the latter course, and I urge that we as a nation learn the lesson of that report and take it as applying to ourselves as well as to the rest of the people in this country. It is a picture of two commanders, unaware of danger. Neglect of duty, if you will; but more than that: It is a picture of the world of routine where the Navy high-hatted the Army and the Army "brass-hatted" the Navy. It is a picture of days in which men thought by passing the buck and writing reports and following the routine practices of a sleepy pre-war day they could discharge their sense of responsibility.

And, in another sense, it is a picture of a whole country—130 million people—many saw the danger but no one acted on it to the limit, and no one to an adequate degree. No one of us can claim exemption from that.

> [The military's report on the Pearl Harbor attack] is a picture of days in which men thought by passing the buck and writing reports and following the routine practices of a sleepy pre-war day they could discharge their sense of responsibility.

Dewey's Advance Warnings

I notice, and took considerable pride from it, that back in 1940 I made two speeches on a national radio hook-up on two days two weeks apart calling for a single head of production in view of the emergency of the nation, and I am sure at least 10,000 others in the intervening 18 months did the same. And yet, that Pearl Harbor state of mind resulted in 18 months of delay before we could get the rudimentary necessities of a national production in the way of an order from the President for a single united command for production for this war.

> There is . . . an uneasy feeling in the minds of many wondering whether there is a whitewash of ultimate responsibility for failure to command more adequate action than the reports showed was actually taking place.

It is a picture of Washington, this report. It is a picture of a Washington working hard. Everybody, you know, down there is working 8, 9, and 10 hours a day, and with a considerable sense of responsibility; and most of us know many people who are down there with a great sense of responsibility. But it is still a picture of a Washington which is living on reports, which is doing a routine and unimaginative routine, while we are opposed to the most imaginative creators of war machines the world has ever seen.

There are some uglier sides. The report shows that there were reports by these two officers, the General and the Admiral, as to exactly what they were doing pursuant to the instructions from Washington, and the reports were well before December 7th, and no criticism came from the high command.

There is, and I think it is a public duty to express it, an uneasy feeling in the minds of many wondering whether there is a whitewash of ultimate responsibility for failure to command more adequate action than the reports showed was actually taking place. It is an amazing picture of espionage, of failure of counter-espionage, of 200 Japanese spies operating out of a Consulate sending thousands of messages over the American system of communications to their head office in Tokio [*sic*], in which they were able to display the entire situation for the benefit of their own high command and without one ounce of interference or even of the interception so far as the report shows of a single message.

A Country Unwilling to Plug Security Leaks

Again, the report gives a picture of those idyllic days when people thought only in terms of their own views about the way a country should be run without any effort to face reality. It recalls the fight in Congress on a bill to attempt to correct what I conceive to have been a judicial misinterpretation of the Communications Act to say that no federal agent, for the protection of the domestic safety of the United States, or of its country, in time of war might intercept any message on any communications system whatsoever for any purpose; and Congress failed to pass the bill permitting that even in felony or espionage cases.

> I regret to say that I think the American nation as a whole is still in a pre-Pearl Harbor condition.

The report is reminiscent of our own State, where in 1938 there was a determined effort by idealistic, well-meaning but grossly misinformed people, led by the Governor of the State, to write a prohibition against such interception of messages into the Constitution of the State of New York; and it was one of the toughest battles I ever saw. And, finally, we succeeded in getting a proper provision written in that such protection for the domestic safety of the State and for the national safety should not be barred, but should be permitted under judicial order. And I am proud to say that at least the State of New York did not make the same blunder that the Federal Government did in that field.

The report leads to many conclusions, but in general it is only fair to say that in all brutal frankness, the Roberts report is a mirror of the entire United States of America on December 7, 1941. It names a General and an Admiral, and it could name every single one of us. I know of no exception, either in public office or in private life, Democrat or Republican, any one of you or me. There can be no exceptions.

Where do we go from here? The real question is: Are we still in a pre-Pearl Harbor state of mind as we sit here in our dinner clothes eating a nice dinner? Is the nation as a whole in that frame of mind? I regret to say that I think the American nation as a whole is still in a pre-Pearl Harbor condition.

Congress Remains Inert in a Time of Crisis

The beginning of August last year [1941] it was already apparent to every thinking person that we were going to have a radical rise in prices, and for six uninterrupted months the Congress of the United States, Republicans and Democrats alike, have been struggling with every bit of influence and power at their command over a price control bill which is still not enacted into law. More than that, a draft has finally been turned out which is wholly unacceptable both to the proponents and to the opponents. No member of Congress would have the effrontery to claim that it is worth the paper it is written on. So far, Congress promises no respectable price control bill.

Meanwhile, the costs of this war and of living are skyrocketing and there seems to be no basic approach to it.

Secondly, yesterday in the papers of the United States there was broadcast a resolution by a dominant labor group in the United States calling upon all component parts of that organization to demand a consistently higher wage rate throughout the year upon the theory

Many Americans assumed wrongly that they would continue to enjoy a rising standard of living, even during a war. As the war continued, many consumer goods became unavailable at any price. (Getty Images.)

that the standard of living would have to continue to rise for those of us who stay home and do not fight.

At the same time, we find minority blocks in the Congress demanding a hundred and twenty per cent of parity for agriculture, which is what no farm leader ever asked. It is an illusion and a fraud, because parity means a relationship between all prices. It is a special privilege which is not desired either by the farmer nor his legitimate leaders. And yet, it has been passed tentatively.

The Illusion of Luxury

And still, we find in industry some groups, who are fortunately very small, who believe the war is a means by which they can get rich off the government.

> And still, we find in industry some groups, who are fortunately very small, who believe the war is a means by which they can get rich off the government.

Basically, there is a total lack of realization, first of all, that we are in a situation where however much money you can lay your hands on won't do you one dime's worth of good. Fifty per cent of all the production of the United States is going to be for war goods, which means that only half of it can be for consumption goods. And yet, they talk about increasing the standard of living. The standard of living in the United States, aside from food and a home, is made up of better clothing, of automobiles, radios, electric refrigerators, the lamps and the rugs and the furniture in your home, and the luxuries of life. Those luxuries aren't going to be manufactured. And this great basic misconception of economics, which lies throughout leadership in group after group of this country, leads them to proclaim that they can raise a living standard by having money to buy goods that don't exist. Millions of Americans are being led down the road of demagoguery to believe that they can grasp after a non-existent thing, the consumption of goods which cannot be manufactured because the manufacturing capacity is engaged in winning a war. We need not only education but a facing of the truth. More money can't buy more goods. All it can do is increase the cost of the war, tend to national bankruptcy, and ultimately burden every one of us infinitely worse after the war.

Our Own Pearl Harbors

I came today, just before I got here, from a meeting of the Trustees of a hospital of which I am a trustee, and in that hospital they are learning that we are in a war. Twenty of the critical items, without which a hospital cannot effectively operate, are today not only unbuyable but unobtainable in the United States for any purpose whatsoever, and that includes medical supplies, gauze, and many drugs. Moreover, within 3 months there will be such a nursing shortage in the City of New York that I venture to prophesy that the private nursing of any patient in any hospital will soon become prohibited as a matter of national emergency.

> "We must be prepared to rebuke selfishness firmly, to educate the people of this country on the real economics of war-time."

Moreover, in servicing units for the army and the navy we are going to strip ourselves of doctors, so that every hospital in the country is going to be short-handed. And yet, throughout the nation we are talking about conducting our affairs as if there were no war.

The Pearl Harbor report, in short, can smother our real defects by creating a couple of scapegoats for us. Or, we can realize that every single person in this country in public life or in private life has a little private Pearl Harbor in his own life.

More than that, the failure to realize our own problems is evidenced in every act of the Congress, because the people have not yet come to face realities and demand it. Sugar rationing is to come, and there is complaining. Whatever the incompetence, we can fight it out, but then learn to like it. We have got to be prepared to support real price fixing. We have got to be prepared to support real rationing, and I am prepared now to advocate that every single item that goes into consumption in this country be rationed because if it isn't the man with the larger income can buy extra suits of clothes; however much the prices be fixed and create an unwholesome atmosphere of favoritism which though not real will undermine national morale. We must be prepared to rebuke selfishness firmly, to educate the people of this country on the real economics of war-time so that they shan't be led down blind alleys, to live in our kitchen, in our home, in our office, and in our daily lives as if we really were at war.

If we have the courage to face reality and to give up gladly the things that we have to give up, if we have the courage to speak the truth, to criticize where it be necessary, to support however much it hurts, we can win this war. We haven't won it yet. It can be lost. We are a long, long way from winning it now. And until every citizen in this country recognizes that he is just as much responsible for Pearl Harbor as those in high office, and they have plenty of responsibility to answer for, we will all have our own private Pearl Harbor, we will all have our own sense of guilt, and if we have the courage to recognize it and to mean it, America will come through this crisis as it always has in the past.

The U.S. Government Did Not Receive Warning Messages Until After the Attack on Pearl Harbor Began

Kendrick Frazier

In the years since the attack on Pearl Harbor, historians and ordinary citizens alike have wondered how the massive assault could have been planned and carried out so successfully without any advance notice by U.S. government or military. While many theories have been submitted for both official and nonofficial review, the belief that the U.S. government withheld intercepted Japanese messages that would have served as warnings has persisted as a possible explanation. In the viewpoint that follows, however, Kendrick Frazier refutes this hypothesis and argues that extensive, recently released reports confirm that

SOURCE. Kendrick Frazier, "The Pearl Harbor 'Winds Message' Controversy: A New Critical Evaluation," *Skeptical Inquirer*, March–April 2009. Reproduced by permission.

the Roosevelt administration did not receive advance warning of the attacks. Frazier contends that warning messages were not transmitted until after the attacks began and, even at that point, did not contain any information that could have changed the course of events. Kendrick Frazier is the editor of the *Skeptical Inquirer* and a fellow at the American Association for the Advancement of Science, an organization dedicated to fostering science, engineering, and innovation throughout the world.

It is not every day that one receives a report in the mail from the supersecret National Security Agency. NSA is the U.S. intelligence agency responsible for the collection and analysis of foreign communications and foreign signals intelligence. And when the report investigates the history of one of the long-disputed contentions about the worst war of the twentieth century, it deserves special attention.

The Japanese attack on Pearl Harbor on December 7, 1941, continues to inspire suspicion in some quarters that the U.S. knew it was coming. Some revisionist and conspiracy writers, historians, and critics of the [Franklin D.] Roosevelt administration contend that the U.S. intercepted a Japanese message that was a clear warning of the impending attack on the U.S. fleet at Pearl Harbor. Some further contend that this so-called "Winds message" had been revealed to senior American military and civilian leaders. The implication is that the attack might therefore have been prevented.

> The Japanese attack on Pearl Harbor on December 7, 1941, continues to inspire suspicion in some quarters that the U.S. knew it was coming.

The story long ago acquired near-mythic status in some circles and has never quite gone away. This group of believers may even have grown in recent years due to the proliferation of Web sites on the Internet with entries about the Winds message.

Historians Refute the "Winds Message"

Historians Robert J. Hanyok and the late David P. Mowry of NSA's Center for Cryptologic History have now published a new, detailed documentary history of the Winds message controversy in an attempt to clear up the issue and provide source documents for historical scholars and researchers. NSA recently issued the 327-page report ("West Wind Clear: Cryptology and the Winds Message Controversy"), which includes images of all the standard critical documents—as well as many never before seen. The authors debunk the view that a clear warning message was monitored before the attacks.

Hanyok told the *Skeptical Inquirer* that he believes his report "will dispel any further reference to a 'Winds execute' message being heard before the attack," at least in conventional and academic circles. He says he holds few such hopes regarding most conspiracy-theory bloggers, unless they actually read the report. "Some conspiracy buffs might change their minds if they read my book."

> Many scholars and researchers have been skeptical or critical of the various revisionist or conspiracist claims revolving around the eventual Winds execute message.

In a foreword, NSA historian David A. Hatch says Hanyok and Mowry "have made a significant contribution to our knowledge and understanding of two of the event's controversies, the Winds Message and the state of U.S. communications intelligence prior to the Hawaiian attack."

Decoding the Winds Message

Japan's coded Winds message was intended by the Japanese foreign ministry as an emergency method to alert Japanese diplomats abroad that relations between Japan and the U.S., Great Britain, or the Soviet Union were about to take a downturn. They could then destroy cryptographic materials or sensitive messages.

One method involved placing innocuous-sounding phrases about the winds in weather forecasts transmitted by short-wave radio. For example, "Nishi No Kaze Hare" ["West Wind Clear"] repeated twice in the middle and twice at the end of the daily Japanese-language short-wave voice news broadcast meant Japan-Great Britain relations were in danger. The phrase "East Wind Rain" signaled damage to U.S. relations. The U.S. intercepted and decrypted the late-November 1941 messages giving these meanings and instructions—as had Great Britain and Australia. Allied monitoring stations were then tasked to search for and monitor any messages bearing these phrases.

Many scholars and researchers have been skeptical or critical of the various revisionist or conspiracist claims revolving around the eventual Winds execute message. Some suggest that the claims are based on a selective reading of testimony and evidence that subsequently surfaced (eight investigations into the Pearl Harbor attacks ensued, from 1942 to 1946). Hanyok and Mowry thought this material might allow them "to examine important aspects of the Winds message story in a deeper fashion than before."

A Useless Warning After the Attack Began

On December 7 in Hawaii, at 1:32 P.M., Honolulu time, five and a half hours *after* the attacks began, a monitoring station on Hawaii heard a Japanese-language news broadcast from Tokyo breathlessly describing the day's attacks by Japanese forces, including a "death-defying raid upon the American naval and air strength in the Hawaiian area." The announcer then interrupted with a weather report: "West Wind Clear" (relations with Great Britain are in danger). He repeated the phrase and did so twice more at the end of the program. This Winds execute message was also monitored at Portland, Oregon, at 7:02 P.M., Eastern Time. It also was: "West Wind Clear." Again, this was hours after the attack. The code phrase referencing relations with the United States was absent from these messages.

Hanyok and Mowry conclude that the Winds message was neither actionable intelligence nor a useful war warning. "A Winds Execute message was sent on 7 December, 1941," the authors say. "The weight of the evidence indicates that one coded phrase, 'West Wind Clear,' was broadcast according to previous instructions some six to seven hours after the attack on Pearl Harbor." They say it is possible that a British site may have heard a broadcast one to two hours after the attack, "but this only substantiates the anticlimatic nature of the broadcast."

"From a military standpoint, the Winds coded message contained no actionable intelligence either about the Japanese operations in Southeast Asia and absolutely nothing about Pearl Harbor. In reality, the Japanese broadcast the coded phrase(s) long after hostilities began—useless, in fact, to all who might have heard it."

The Making of a Conspiracy Theory

They further find that the controversy was in fact an artificial one, pumped up by misunderstandings and the imaginings of one of the key participants, whose narratives "ranged so far from the documentary evidence and the memories of all the other participants that it was completely detached from actual events." And they say revisionist and conspiratorial writers since then have further strayed from the documented truth.

"There simply was not one shred of actionable intelligence in any of the messages or transmissions that pointed to the attack on Pearl Harbor."

The "primary, and almost exclusive, source fueling these claims of a conspiracy surrounding the Winds message," say the authors, was Captain Laurance Frye Safford, the founder and first commander of the U.S.

Navy's code-breaking unit, OP-20-G. Safford first publicized his views in early 1944 in the Hart Inquiry, the second of the eight investigations after the attack. He repeated his story in Army Board and Navy Board investigations later that same year. He was well regarded within the cryptologic and intelligence communities and therefore taken seriously.

In their report's final section, "The Winds Message and the Historical Process," Hanyok and Mowry are highly critical of Safford and later conspiratorial writers.

"The 'conspiratorial' version of the Winds incident was solely the product of Captain Laurance Safford's imagining of events that had occurred prior to Pearl Harbor in the Washington, D.C., offices of naval and army intelligence," say the authors.

A monitoring station on Hawaii did not receive the Japanese broadcast touting the attack on Pearl Harbor until five and a half hours after the attack. The lack of warning resulted in the USS *Arizona*'s destruction. (**AP Images**.)

"Put to the test, though, Safford's narrative about the Execute message simply failed to stand up to cross-examination. The Joint Congressional Committee shredded Safford's story. The committee reduced it to the collection of unsubstantiated charges that all along had been its foundation. The documentary evidence he said was available simply did not, nor did it ever, exist. In truth, Safford produced nothing upon which any further investigation could proceed." They say the most charitable assessment of his actions was that he was "mistaken."

The Resurrection of a Conspiracy Theory

The story should have ended there, the authors say. But thirty-four years after the congressional committee report in 1946, a few private scholars resurrected Safford's allegation of a conspiracy and with it the whole Winds controversy. These writers "inverted the normal rules of evidentiary argument," insisting that "the government had yet to disprove Safford's charges regardless of the fact that he never had produced any evidence to substantiate them thirty-some years earlier," say Hanyok and Mowry.

"The scholars and researchers who championed Safford's version of the controversy abandoned the rigorous evidentiary requirements of the historical profession in order to advance their thesis. . . .

"Safford's case was built on mistaken deductions, reconstructed, nonexistent documents, a mutable version of events, as well as a cast of witnesses that Safford conjured up in his imagination.

"In the end, the Winds message controversy was and remains an artificial historical phenomenon. . . . The artificial controversy that grew around the Winds message never advanced historical knowledge of the events of early December 1941. In fact, the Winds controversy distracted investigations and later historical analyses from far more important issues about the attack on Pearl Harbor." These include, the authors say, "the fundamental organizational and operational shortcomings of American cryptology" and the "arrogant dismissal by American military and naval leaders of a Japanese capability and willingness to conduct such an operation."

"That the Winds controversy persisted over decades is more a result of the misplaced belief by some that history is controlled by conspiracy than history being the product of human folly."

A Comfortable and Comforting Ideology

Hanyok told the *Skeptical Inquirer* that if there is anything he wanted to add to his book it would have been on "Captain Safford's reason behind his dogged persistence in pushing his conspiracy theory." Says Hanyok: "I came across some additional material after my book was at the printer. Safford firmly believed that radio intelligence could discover what the Japanese were up to. He was absolutely certain that the intelligence that tipped off the attack on Pearl Harbor was somewhere in the files of the Navy or Army. When he could not find what he was sure existed, he began to suspect that the files had been picked. So the vague sense of conspiracy came first. Then he began to fit the 'pieces,' no matter how untenable they were, to the story."

He says some "conspiracy bloggers" have already dismissed his book as the work of "court historians." This, he says, is "a curious insult considering that I blew the whistle on the Gulf of Tonkin coverup!" Says Hanyok: "This group is so committed that they will never change their collective mind. Believing in a conspiratorial view of history is a comfortable and comforting ideology."

President Roosevelt Did Not Provoke the Japanese Attack on Pearl Harbor

Kevin Baker

> In the following viewpoint, Kevin Baker argues that attempts to exonerate Admiral Husband E. Kimmel and Major General Walter Short from their share of the blame for the failure at Pearl Harbor are wrongheaded. Baker asserts that the Hawaiian commanders were given enough military intelligence and government warnings to prompt them to a greater level of readiness than they exhibited. Baker further refutes claims that the Franklin D. Roosevelt administration purposefully withheld vital intelligence so that Japan's initial attack would be successful, thus forcing the United States into the war—Roosevelt's supposed aim. Baker suggests that there would be other, less costly ways of getting the U.S. into the war and that attempts to pin the blame for the Pearl Harbor attack on the president are simply byprod-

SOURCE. Kevin Baker, "Another Day of Infamy," *American Heritage*, vol. 52, April 2001. Copyright © 2001 American Heritage Publishing. All rights reserved. Reproduced by permission.

ucts of a modern attitude that takes satisfaction in conspiracy theories and the mistaken belief that those in power are always seeking to cover up the truth. Kevin Baker is a writer and editor whose history-related columns have appeared in the *New York Times*, *American Heritage*, and the *Chicago Tribune*.

What is history? Is it something we decide on the best available evidence, weighing and culling the many varied accounts of the past? Or is it, instead, something to be decreed and imposed on us, decided by what some politicians say or maybe a judge somewhere? These questions may seem banal or obvious, but they have become very real—ever since the U.S. Congress recently decided to write the main tenet of a conspiracy theory into an official bill.

The amendment in question was tacked onto a defense bill and passed by both houses of Congress last October [2000]. It calls on the President [George W. Bush] to restore Rear Adm. Husband E. Kimmel and Maj. Gen. Walter C. Short posthumously to the highest ranks they held at the onset of World War II.

Kimmel and Short were, respectively, the Navy and Army commanders at Pearl Harbor at the time of the Japanese sneak attack there; they were demoted upon their subsequent forced retirements. Asking to restore their ranks is the most, legally, that our national legislature can do. The final decision will rest with the President. Congress would like him to exculpate both men, because they "were not provided necessary and critical intelligence . . . that would have alerted them to prepare for the attack."

Passing the Buck for the Disaster

This last line is the rub. It passes the buck for the fiasco at Pearl Harbor to the high command in Washington at the time, most prominently President Franklin D. Roosevelt and Army Chief of Staff Gen. George C. Marshall. In so doing, it gives credence to the very ur-conspiracy theory of American history, the notion that Roosevelt or Marshall or both knew the Japanese attack was coming but deliberately kept the Pearl Harbor garrison in the dark, in order to maneuver America into World War II.

The backers of the bill have insisted that they are not passing on blame to any particular person or persons. Former Delaware senator William V. Roth, Jr., the amendment's main sponsor, claims that what happened at Pearl Harbor "was a systemic failure in which the gravest mistakes were made by the Washington authorities." But this is disingenuous, at best—a clever political maneuver that makes for bad history. If "critical intelligence" was indeed withheld in Washington, intentionally or not, wasn't *someone* to blame for the loss of 2,403 American lives on December 7, 1941, the "date that will live in infamy"?

> Washington *did* pass on ample warnings that war might be imminent.

A series of military and congressional investigations in the 1940s sought to answer this very question. Their general conclusions were the same as those of a 1995 Pentagon review, which determined that responsibility for the defense of Pearl Harbor that terrible day "should be broadly shared" but that "the intelligence available to Adm. Kimmel and Gen. Short was sufficient to justify a higher level of vigilance than they chose to maintain."

Washington Alerted the Hawaiian Commanders

The vast majority of historians concur, and they are supported by the facts. There was plenty of infamy to go around for Pearl Harbor. The high command in Washington did blunder in not sharing every last scrap of information it had with Kimmel and Short. For that matter, even a garrison that knew the very moment of the Japanese attack would have had trouble resisting it, what with our unforgivable lack of preparedness more than two years after the rest of the world had marched off to war.

Yet Washington *did* pass on ample warnings that war might be imminent. On October 16, 1941, the Office of the Chief of Naval Operations (OPNAV) sent a message to Kimmel advising him that a new cabinet in Japan was likely to be "strongly nationalistic and antiAmerican." It advised that "hostilities between Japan and Russia are a strong possibility" and went on to warn, "Since the US and Britain are held responsible by Japan for her present desperate situation there is also a possibility that Japan may attack these two powers. In view of these possibilities you will take due precautions. . . ."

A further Navy Department message, received by Kimmel on November 27, was even more explicit, beginning: "This despatch is to be considered a war warning. Negotiations with Japan looking toward stabilization of conditions in the Pacific have ceased and an aggressive move by Japan is expected within the next few days." This message stated that the most likely target of a Japanese attack would be "either the Philippines Thai or Kra Peninsula or possibly Borneo" but ordered Kimmel to "execute an appropriate defensive deployment preparatory to carrying out the tasks assigned in WPL [War Plan] 46. Inform district and army authorities. A similar warning is being sent by War Department. . . ."

Finally, on December 3, 1941, the Office of the Chief of Naval Operations warned Kimmel that Japanese diplomats in London, Hong Kong, Singapore, Manila, and Washington had been instructed to destroy their top code machines "and all secret documents." Remarkably, Kimmel would later testify that he did not consider the destruction of the code machines to be "of any vital importance." Indeed, no warnings of any sort, from either

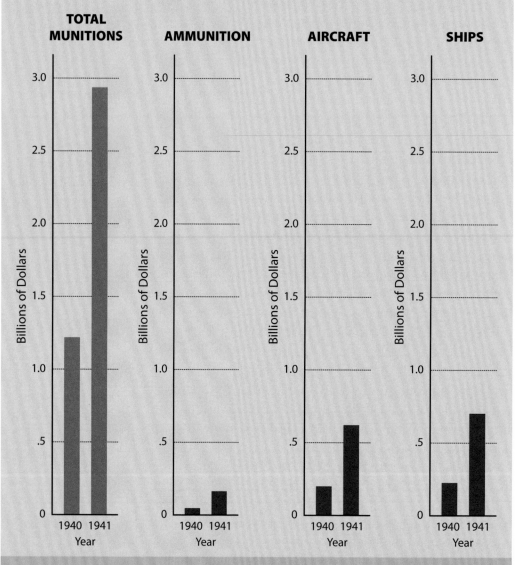

MUNITIONS PRODUCTION PRIOR TO PEARL HARBOR

These graphs show fourth-quarter war production in 1940 and 1941. The substantial increase in 1941 expenditures indicates that the United States was building its defense capabilities at an accelerated rate in the year prior to entering the war.

TOTAL MUNITIONS

AMMUNITION

AIRCRAFT

SHIPS

Taken from: *The United States at War: Development and Administration of the War Program by the Federal Government.* Washington, DC: Government Printing Office, 1947.

Washington or their *own* intelligence officers, moved Short and Kimmel to take any special precautions.

On December 6, the very eve of the Japanese attack, General Short was informed that the Japanese consulate in Honolulu was burning *its* papers, something his chief intelligence officer regarded as "very significant." Short later recalled receiving the information but "did not consider it a matter of importance."

On the morning of December 7, about an hour before the Japanese planes struck, Kimmel was informed that his ships had sunk a Japanese minisub trying to enter Pearl Harbor.

One is tempted to be flippant and ask, "Just what part of 'This despatch is to be considered a war warning' didn't you understand?" but that would be unfair. Few people can even begin to comprehend what it must be like to command a large base in time of war. The constant barrage of information received in such circumstances, most of it scurrilous or irrelevant, can obscure what seems, with the advantage of hindsight, to be the most direct of warnings. What these messages do make clear, however, is the weakness of the conspiracy theories surrounding Pearl Harbor. If Franklin Roosevelt or anyone else in Washington had wanted Pearl Harbor caught by surprise, why pass on such direct advisories to the base there? Why, for that matter, would any Commander in Chief want his forces caught napping in the first place? All Washington had to do was to give Pearl Harbor an explicit last-minute warning and Japan's fleet would have been caught flatfooted, thousands of miles from its home waters and close to nothing but American possessions. A sneak attack in which Americans ably defended them-

> If Franklin Roosevelt or anyone else in Washington had wanted Pearl Harbor caught by surprise, why pass on such direct advisories to the base there? Why, for that matter, would any Commander in Chief want his forces caught napping in the first place?

A U.S. Admiral Asserts That President Roosevelt Was Bent on War

The bait offered Japan was our Pacific fleet. In 1940, Admiral J.O. Richardson, the fleet's commander, flew to Washington to protest [Franklin Delano Roosevelt's] decision to permanently base the fleet in Hawaii instead of its normal berthing on the U.S. West Coast. The admiral had sound reasons: Pearl Harbor was vulnerable to attack, being approachable from any direction; it could not be effectively rigged with nets and baffles to defend against torpedo planes; and in Hawaii it would be hard to supply and train crews for his undermanned vessels. Pearl Harbor also lacked adequate fuel supplies and dry docks, and keeping men far from their families would create morale problems. The argument became heated. Said Richardson:

"I came away with the impression that, despite his spoken word, the President was fully determined to put the United States into the war if Great Britain could hold out until he was reelected."

Richardson was quickly relieved of command. Replacing him was Admiral Husband E. Kimmel. Kimmel also informed Roosevelt of Pearl Harbor's deficiencies, but accepted placement there, trusting that Washington would notify him of any intelligence pointing to attack. This proved to be misplaced trust. As Washington watched Japan preparing to assault Pearl Harbor, Admiral Kimmel, as well as his Army counterpart in Hawaii, General Walter C. Short, were completely sealed off from the information pipeline.

SOURCE. *James Perloff, "Pearl Harbor: Hawaii Was Surprised; FDR Was Not,"* New American, *December 4, 2008.* *www.thenewamerican.com.*

selves and beat back the attackers would have looked far better for the President—and still got us into war.

The Administration Tried to Forestall War

Yet any objective look at the historical record shows that far from trying to provoke a war in the Pacific, the Roosevelt administration was doing its best to forestall one. FDR and his closest advisers had always viewed [Adolf] Hitler and Nazi Germany as the leading threat to the United States, and they feared that the country would be distracted from this menace by a war with Japan.

True, Germany was supposed to come to Japan's aid under the terms of the Axis pact, but then, Hitler was hardly known for honoring his treaties. Roosevelt actually pursued what amounted to a stalling strategy in Asia for months, alternating economic embargoes with conciliatory negotiations. Obviously, the policy was a failure, but it was nevertheless one that FDR pursued right up to the end, sending a direct last-ditch appeal for peace to Emperor Hirohito on December 6.

> It is, in the end, disturbing that one even has to debunk this sort of libel against men like Franklin Roosevelt and George Marshall.

Indeed, Roosevelt's "date that will live in infamy" speech to Congress asks for a declaration of war only against Japan. Even with that there might have been some difficulty in getting us into the war in Europe had Hitler not been arrogant enough to beat us to the punch, declaring war on the United States on December 11.

It is, in the end, disturbing that one even has to debunk this sort of libel against men like Franklin Roosevelt and George Marshall. Certainly, history is an ongoing process of revision and debate, and mistrust of any received wisdom can be a good thing. Yet most of the promulgators of conspiracy theories are not engaging in anything like a serious historical debate. Rather they are using a whole series of other forums—shoddy television shows, sensational movies such as [director and screenwriter] Oliver Stone's ongoing chronicles of American paranoia, and now legal and political actions—to push their propaganda across without serious scrutiny.

In November and December 1999, to take another example, the family of the late Reverend Dr. Martin

U.S. president Franklin D. Roosevelt considered German dictator Adolf Hitler (front row, center) and his military aggressions in Europe to be the largest threats to the United States and viewed Japan as a potential distraction. Here, Hitler marches with ally Benito Mussolini (front row, right) in Munich. (DEA Picture Library.)

Luther King, Jr., used a wrongful-death suit to press their belief that Dr. King was assassinated not by James Earl Ray but by a much wider government conspiracy, one possibly orchestrated by President Lyndon Johnson. The Kings' lawyer, a longtime conspiracy theorist, exploited the opportunity to fill an official court record with all sorts of innuendo and speculation about the civil rights leader's death. He thereby pre-empted a thorough new Justice Department investigation, begun in 1998 and concluded last June [2000], that found no evidence of a government conspiracy.

Decimating History to Benefit Political Agendas

"These are historical judgments rendered without evidence or meaning," was how Ambassador William vanden Heuvel, chairman of the Franklin and Eleanor

Roosevelt Institute, characterized both the King "trial" and the congressional resolution for Kimmel and Short. Which also brings us back to our original question: What is history? It is all that we are now, and all that we believe ourselves to be? If we are to start now tearing ourselves down, knocking apart everything we know to be the truth, not on the basis of any new evidence or research but simply to serve some narrow purpose or ancient grudge, what will be left of us? Wouldn't that reduce us to a nation of seething suspicion, bereft of a common reality? If the U.S. Congress were to pass a resolution claiming that Husband Kimmel and Walter Short were dedicated, patriotic men who served their country to their best of their ability and should not be singled out for censure—if it were to declare that they did no worse than, say, even such a commander as Douglas MacArthur [commander of U.S. military forces in the Pacific], who was caught with his planes on the ground in the Philippines the day *after* Pearl Harbor—then I, for one, would have nothing against restoring them to their full ranks, and I suspect that nearly all Americans would feel the same way.

Or, if the Congress really does believe that "critical intelligence" was withheld from the garrison at Pearl Harbor, it ought to hold fair and balanced hearings on the matter and lay out all its findings to the public. To conduct its business as it has is to sneak a conspiracy theory through the back door of the people's house. It sets a sorry precedent.

Japanese Naval Blunders Followed the Pearl Harbor Attack

Masataka Chihaya

Following the Japanese success at Pearl Harbor, the United States Navy was crippled and vulnerable. In the viewpoint that follows, Japanese historian Masataka Chihaya contends that Japan should have committed to a second, immediate attack on the ground in Hawaii to inflict more, lasting damage on the U.S. fleet and land bases. Further, he argues that the overconfidence shown by the Japanese political and military leaders hindered them from honestly assessing the conflict and planning appropriately for future battles. Thus, Masataka comes to the conclusion that while it was a great singular victory for Japan, Pearl Harbor served as the impetus for the United States to resolutely enter the war, rebuild, and reassess their naval forces and strategy and eventually turn the tide of war. Masataka Chihaya was an officer in the Japanese navy and completed this assessment

SOURCE. Masataka Chihaya, *The Pearl Harbor Papers: Inside the Japanese Plans*. Dulles, VA: Brassey's, 2000. Copyright © 1993 by Prange Enterprises, Inc. All rights reserved. Reproduced by permission of Potomac Books, Inc. (formerly Brassey's Inc.).

of his country's forces in the decade following the end of World War II.

On 26 November 1941 our fleet [the Japanese] started from Hitokappu Bay of the Kurile Island group. It sailed due east across the Pacific. The waves were high. At dawn of [7] December, from the north of the Hawaii islands flew 360-odd planes up into still-dark skies and dashed a surprise attack on the American Pacific Fleet anchored there and the air forces. The result was brilliant. We succeeded in destroying the greater part of the American airplanes and most of the larger units of the American navy that happened to be there. On our part the loss was negligible indeed. We lost only 29 aircraft and one submarine engaged in scouting at the mouth of the harbor. As a battle it was an unrivalled success; however, the value was questionable from the war standpoint, as a way to start a war against Great America.

> "The navy had become a violator of international law. This single circumstance was fatal to Japan's honor on the one hand, while it aroused the martial spirit of the entire American people, adding infinitely to their fighting power."

Japan Awakens a Sleeping Giant

The attack was to be started after the declaration of war. But due to some impediment in communications, it has actually turned out to be an attack without notice, just a sneak attack and was branded as such. The navy had become a violator of international law. This single circumstance was fatal to Japan's honor on the one hand, while it aroused the martial spirit of the entire American people, adding infinitely to their fighting power. In the impact on the American mind, "Remember the *Maine*" [a rallying cry for the United States to enter into war against

Spain after the battleship *Maine* was sunk in Havana harbor in February 1898] must have paled into nothingness as compared with "Remember Pearl Harbor." At the moment when the leaders of the navy devised such a tactic, did it occur to any single one of them for one single moment how such a mode of attack would work on the American mind?

Then did they utilize the result of the first attack for the subsequent operations of the war? In the first place,

Admiral Chuichi Nagumo led Japanese forces in the raid on Pearl Harbor on December 7, 1941. Nagumo withdrew from the battle after only a single coup, which may have been a grave military error. (**Time & Life Pictures/Getty Images.**)

why did they not follow it up with a close second? And a third? Was a landing possible?

Japan Decides Against a Second Attack

At the time of the outbreak I was serving as a staff member in charge of the construction of the so-called "Hope of Japan," the battleship *Musashi* at Nagasaki of later atomic bomb fame. When I heard over the radio of the attack on Pearl Harbor, my whole nerve just tingled. I remember indulging in a discussion on the above-mentioned two points with some of my friends. One conclusion was that they should have followed the advantage without letting the enemy catch its breath. As it actually was, this did not take place. Admiral [Chuichi] Nagumo, who then commanded the task force, gathered the units and withdrew from the battle areas without trying a second coup. Why such a course of tactics? The reasons may be guessed as follows:

1. First was the problem of fuel. Of the units taking part in the attack, those that could operate on their own fuel supply were only the carriers *Kaga*, *Shokaku* and *Zuikaku*, the battleships *Hiei* and *Kirishima*, the cruisers *Tone* and *Chikuma*. As regards the light cruisers such as the *Abukuma* and the destroyers, it had been planned to give them up in midocean in case fuel could not be replenished at sea. This difficulty besetting the fuel supply was certainly one of the important causes that prevented the navy from carrying out the second attack on Hawaii.

2. The lost airplanes were only 29, but the damaged ones that called for repair were pretty many. We did not have ready sufficient numbers with which to deliver the second attack. In other words, our navy had thought of just one attack.

3. "We have given a crushing blow. We have made a record which is enough. The adventure of the second attack is not worth the risk, is not necessary." This is the

> **Our navy felt their business was through.**

philosophy. They thought and argued in altogether Japanese fashion, the mentality of our champion wrestler in the national *Sumo* game, triumphantly retiring amid handslaps and acclamation from the ring. Just like a wrestler in such a position, our navy felt their business was through. They were playing a game, just sporting. A chase, a pursuit—such ideas were entirely alien to their minds. This will furnish the answer to the question why they did not undertake a landing. They had not even dreamed of it.

Japan's Navy Fails to Learn from Both Victories and Mistakes

In reaping the full harvest of a victory the navy's thought lacked thoroughness and perfection in such a way. Much

The Tide Changes After Months of "Running Wild"

Though the first six months of the Pacific War bore bitter tidings for Americans, in spring 1942 the fortunes of Japan began to change. The master plan drawn up by Adm. Isoroku Yamamoto—to inflict maximum damage on the American navy in order to buy precious time to negotiate—was thwarted by the unpredictable. On the morning of 7 December 1941 the aircraft carriers at Pearl Harbor, the heart of the American fleet, were at sea. Their destruction had been the most important aspect of the Japanese war aims because without them American military operations in the Pacific would have no air support. With its carriers intact the United States could strike back much more quickly than Yamamoto desired. He had told his superiors that he could "run wild" for the first six months or year of war, but he had no confidence for the second and third years. In May 1942 his prediction began to prove true. When a Japanese carrier force threatened the Allied air base at Port Moresby, New Guinea, the Battle of the Coral Sea became the first naval less did it occur to them to derive useful lessons from such experiences for future improvement. They never did mercilessly, critically, thoroughly pass this great experience under severe examination and appraise the results. On the contrary, it may even be said this spectacular victory even poisoned the navy's mind and put it on the track of their final undoing. The victory was so great that the elation expelled victory irrevocably.

Two days later, on 10 December off Malay, the navy's air forces attacked the *Prince of Wales*, the British dreadnought flying the flag of Admiral Phillips, and the *Repulse*, with the remarkable success of sinking both of them almost instantly. This phenomenal success has demonstrated the enormous values of the air forces and the task forces. It meant a revolution in naval warfare. But has our navy continued their effort in this direction further on? Alas, no! They made some endeavors to

engagement in history in which ships did not fire on each other. Rather, the entire battle took place between planes based on the carriers of each fleet. The result was a decisive U.S. victory, made possible by the presence of the American carriers not destroyed at Pearl Harbor. Though the U.S.S. *Lexington* was destroyed, it and the *Yorktown* put three Japanese carriers out of commission and prevented any further Japanese expansion southward to Australia. The following month, at the Battle of Midway, with Japan's capi-tal carriers missing, the United States broke the entire Japanese naval initiative. From then on Tokyo would fight a completely defensive war.

SOURCE. *"World War II: The Pacific Campaign, 1941–1945," DISCovering U.S. History. Gale Research, 1997. Reproduced in History Resource Center. Farmington Hills, MI: Gale. http://galenet.galegroup. com/servlet/HistRC.*

increase the production of airplanes, but not of carriers. The serious effort to increase the carriers started after the loss of the *Akagi*, *Kaga*, *Soryu* and *Hiryu* in the attack on Midway [approximately six months after the Pearl Harbor attack]. Only after this terrific disaster did they set about building carriers with bloodshot eyes.

As I have mentioned already, at the time of the Pearl Harbor attack I was in Nagasaki serving as a staff member attending to the construction of the battleship *Musashi*. Alongside, the *Izumo Maru*, the would-be Japan's No. 1 passenger steamer, was being converted into a carrier named *Junyo*. The naval staff and all the personnel of the dockyard engaged in the building of this latter had to make room, so to speak, for those engaged in the construction of the battleship *Musashi*. The latter looked so much more important, carried in the consciousness they were attending to a job of minor importance so much more prestige. The demonstration beyond dispute of the tremendous value of the carriers in those two memorable engagements did not destroy this complex. The navy's mind was so slow to change, the slave of inertia!

> We felt deeply struck by the excellently scientific attitude with which the American government has treated this problem.

Further, they had made no very serious study in the operation of the task forces. In other words, they admitted nothing but the anthem of the "Irresistible Imperial navy" that began to be chanted in a general sort of way all over Japan since 1940. They became simply puffed up, self-conceited, vain, a damned fool. The great superiority of the different types of aircraft that took part in the attack on Pearl Harbor could be admitted. There were perhaps no matches for them in the entire world about this time. But the excessive confidence in their abilities soon changed into making light of others and the evaporation of the spirit of emulation.

The U.S. Navy Benefits from Defeat

Against this, what did the American navy learn? At the time we could know nothing except the relieving of Admiral Kimmel of his post and the opening of the Investigation Committee to pry into the cause of the Pearl Harbor disaster. But the subsequent activities of the American sea forces all over the Pacific area are quite eloquent of what lessons the American navy learned from this experience. One year after the signing of the armistice, reading the announcement by the Pearl Harbor Investigation Committee of the result of their investigations we felt deeply struck by the excellently scientific attitude with which the American government has treated this problem. Our complete defeat was in the due course of matter. Now that we can account for our defeat, we have behaved just to concede the victory to the Americans. If our navy had been in America's place, would they have taken the attitude the Americans did take? By all means, No!

We scored a victory of which we could well be proud, but subsequently we committed a blunder that more than offset the brilliance of the early victory. America, [which] had suffered a terrible calamity at first, secured from it a moral benefit that far outweighed the material damages.

The Lessons of Pearl Harbor Drove Cold War Policy in the United States

Takuya Sasaki

The significance of any given historical event often reaches beyond a country's reactions at the time. In the viewpoint that follows, Japanese historian Takuya Sasaki explores one facet of the lasting U.S. foreign policy implications of the attack on Pearl Harbor. Sasaki focuses specifically on U.S. behavior during the Cold War and how government decisions were informed by its memory of unpreparedness in the face of foreign aggression during that "day of infamy." In particular, the author argues that the United States sought to both avoid partaking in a similar type of unannounced attack on the Soviet Union or other Cold War adversary and to ensure it was never again the victim of a

SOURCE. Takuya Sasaki, *The Unpredictability of the Past: Memories of the Asia-Pacific War in U.S.-East Asian Relations*. Durham, NC: Duke University Press, 2007. Copyright 2007, Duke University Press. All rights reserved. Used by permission of the publisher.

stealth assault on its own soil. Takuya Sasaki is a professor in the department of law and politics at Rikkyo University in Tokyo, Japan.

For the American people, the Pacific War was a good war in many ways. The United States entered it by way of Japan's "sneak" attack on Pearl Harbor, fought it for democratic principles against a totalitarian regime, and won a decisive victory. The war confirmed America's own self-image that it was on the right side of history. Being converted to internationalism, the American people grew fully confident of taking an active foreign policy abroad in the postwar world.

Also, Americans became convinced that sufficient military preparedness was the critical element in defending national security. While in the interwar years the United States had mainly relied on economic, financial, and cultural rather than military measures to promote the national interest and international stability, the Pacific War demonstrated the absolute validity of military power in maintaining world peace.

Pearl Harbor was one of two decisive events . . . that shaped the basic assumption of postwar American national security policy. The Japanese surprise attack demonstrated not only that isolationism was no longer tenable but also that constant vigilance against a hostile power and a strong military establishment in peace-time were indispensable. Preventing another Pearl Harbor-type of attack became the foremost task for American policymakers. . . .

> *Preventing another Pearl Harbor-type of attack became the foremost task for American policymakers.*

The U.S. Defense Budget During the Cold War

Paul H. Nitze [a high-ranking U.S. government official], who was soon to become the very embodiment of the postwar national security policy, visited Hiroshima and Nagasaki in the fall of 1945 as a member of the United States Strategic Bombing Survey. After the survey, Nitze submitted a summary report on the Pacific War, wherein he emphasized the need for civil defense measures, scientific research and development, effective intelligence capabilities, unification of the armed forces, and the maintenance of military strength. Nitze referred to the lesson of Pearl Harbor in the concluding part of the report: "The Japanese would have never attacked Pearl Harbor had they not correctly assessed the weakness of our defenses in the Pacific and had they not incorrectly assessed the fighting determination of the United States when attacked." Nitze's summary report on the Pacific War was important since it could be regarded as the forerunner of NSC [National Security Council] 68 and NSC 5724 (the Gaither Report), two significant NSC documents in cold war history. Nitze turned out to be the principal figure who drafted these NSC papers.

> Obviously, Pearl Harbor cast a moral restraint on the conduct of American foreign relations.

In NSC 68 of April 1950, Nitze argued for an immediate, large-scale buildup of conventional and nuclear forces, the cost of which, he estimated, would reach approximately $50 billion annually. This figure was more than three times the defense budget for fiscal 1950. Interestingly, Nitze claimed that the military expansion proposed in NSC 68 was not only a realistic way to counter the mounting military threat of the Soviet Union but was also an alternative to a surprise attack against the Soviet Union. In rejecting a preventive war, NSC 68 pointed out that such a course would be morally "repugnant" and "corrosive" to many Americans. The implication was clear: the United States had a moral obligation to refrain from launching a Pearl Harbor–type of attack. Obviously,

Pearl Harbor cast a moral restraint on the conduct of American foreign relations.

The Blueprint for National Security Policy

In pleading for a dramatic increase in military spending in NSC 68, Nitze cited the economic lesson of World War II: "In an emergency the United States could devote upward of 50 percent of its gross product to these purposes [military expenditures, foreign assistance, and military investment] (as it did during the last war). . . . One of the most significant lessons of our World War II experience was that the American economy, when it operates at a level approaching full efficiency, can provide enormous resources for purposes other than civilian consump-

Russia's launch of the Sputnik I satellite in 1957 was a decisive moment in the Cold War and was viewed by the United States as analogous to the sneak attack on Pearl Harbor. (AFP/Getty Images.)

tion while simultaneously providing a high standard of living." The Korean War, which broke out before long, pushed the defense budget up to $50 billion without seriously hurting the economy, an evolution that apparently bore out the analysis of NSC 68.

In November 1957, Nitze reiterated the gist of NSC 68 in NSC 5724, which offered a highly critical assessment of the [Dwight D.] Eisenhower administration's containment policy. Rejecting the administration's fiscal conservatism, Nitze again pointed out the economic expansion during World War II: "This country is now devoting 8.5% of its production to defense, and 10% to all national security programs. The American people have always been ready to shoulder heavy costs for their defense when convinced of their necessity. We devoted 41% of our gnp [gross national product] to defense at the height of World War II and 14% during the Korean War."

Those who participated in the making of the Gaither Report were prominent bipartisan figures like Robert Lovett, John McCloy, William Foster, and Nitze. This document formed the blueprint of national security policy for the coming Democratic administration, in which all of them were to serve in various capacities.

> In the heyday of the cold war, Pearl Harbor also provided policymakers with a symbolic and useful metaphor for explaining to the public the grave international situation.

Pearl Harbor as a Policy Tool

In the heyday of the cold war, Pearl Harbor also provided policymakers with a symbolic and useful metaphor for explaining to the public the grave international situation; Pearl Harbor had metamorphosed into a convenient policy tool for government officials. In the late 1950s, when the Soviet military threat seemed to rise sharply, the most frequent comparison to be used was Pearl Harbor. As early as June 1955, Senators Henry

Jackson and Clinton Anderson, warning in a letter to President Eisenhower that Soviet possession of an intercontinental ballistic missile could well lead to a "nuclear Pearl Harbor," demanded that he should put the missile program on a "wartime footing" and give it the highest national priority.

Then, in October 1957, the Soviets launched *Sputnik*, the world's first artificial satellite. In the wake of this shocking news, Edward Teller, the father of the h-bomb, commented that the United States had lost "a battle more important and greater than Pearl Harbor." Senator W. Stuart Symington of the Senate Armed Services Committee described *Sputnik* as a "technical Pearl Harbor" and asserted that the Soviet satellite refuted the Eisenhower administration's claim that the United States maintained a qualitative military lead over the Soviet Union. Lyndon Johnson, Senate majority leader, stated in his opening remarks in the Senate hearings, "We meet today in the atmosphere of another Pearl Harbor." Joseph W. Alsop, one of the most influential journalists in the postwar period, observed in his January 1960 column that the United States was lagging behind the Soviets in missile capabilities and warned that "something much worse than Pearl Harbor can now be the result."

Even President Eisenhower, who emphatically refuted the Pearl Harbor analogy in the missile gap controversy, resorted to this metaphor in defending a secret aerial reconnaissance over Soviet territory. When the U-2 affair [in which a U.S. U-2 spy plane was shot down over the Soviet Union] aborted his visit to Moscow in May 1960, Eisenhower justified the spy mission by saying in a press conference, "No one wants another Pearl Harbor."

Pearl Harbor and the Cuban Missile Crisis

The Pearl Harbor analogy was again frequently invoked during the Cuban Missile Crisis [a confrontation between the U.S. and the Soviet Union in October 1962], which brought the two superpowers closer to nuclear war than any other crisis in the cold war years. According to Ernest R. May and Philip D. Zelikow:

> In the debates recorded on [John F.] Kennedy's tapes, Pearl Harbor has a presence [. . .]. Absent Pearl Harbor, the whole debate about the Soviet missiles in Cuba might have been different. . . . Most important of all, Pearl Harbor served as a conclusive example of the proposition that a secretive government might pursue its ambitions, or relieve its frustrations, by adopting courses of action that objectively seemed irrational or even suicidal. This proposition haunts discussion of Soviet motives and possible Soviet reactions during the missile crisis.

Secretary of State Dean Rusk later recalled that when he heard the Federal Bureau of Investigation report that Soviet diplomats were destroying sensitive documents at their embassy in Washington, it reminded him that Japanese diplomats had burned documents the night before Pearl Harbor. On the other hand, some Ex Comm (Executive Committee of the National Security Council) members worried about "a Pearl Harbor in reverse." Under Secretary of State George Ball, for instance, argued that a prompt air strike was a kind of attack that the Soviet Union might carry out. Similarly, Attorney General Robert Kennedy explained that such an attack was "not in our traditions." His remark infuriated Dean Acheson, who believed the analogy was inappropriate because the president repeatedly warned against installment of the nuclear weapon in the hemisphere. Nonetheless, apparently touching the nerves of other participants in the Ex Comm, Kennedy's warning was instrumental in winning their support for the naval blockade. As NSC 68 had predicted, moral inhibitions figured prominently in the ultimate rejection of a preventive war strike like Pearl Harbor.

The Pearl Harbor Memorial Is a Space of Conflicting Histories

Liz Reed

In the viewpoint that follows, Liz Reed recounts her visit to the war memorial established on the site of the sinking of the USS *Arizona* at Pearl Harbor. In her opinion, the memorial is a "performance of remembering," a set of cultural codes that invite— even expect—visitors to participate in a shared narrative that portrays the United States as a non-aggressor sneakily attacked by a foe that was already bent on acquiring assets and resources in the Pacific that were vital to U.S. security. For Reed, this narrative seems to resonate with the pro-American narrative the U.S. government has used to characterize the September 11, 2001, terrorist attacks and justify the subsequent invasion of Iraq. Reed believes the war memorial might be better conceived of as a peace memorial, one that reminds visitors that militarism is still part of U.S. history and that global unity is not yet

SOURCE. Liz Reed, "Manifest Destiny: The Pearl Harbour Memorial Becomes a Contested Space on the Eve of War," *Arena*, April-May 2003, pp. 24–25. Copyright 2003 Arena Printing and Publications Pty. Ltd. Reproduced by permission.

a reality. Liz Reed works in the Centre for Australian Indigenous Studies at Monash University in Melbourne.

Visit the Pearl Harbor website and you will read how the USS *Arizona* Memorial "as a national shrine symbolises American sacrifice and resolve", and how the sneaky attack by the Japanese on the morning of 7 December 1941 "awoke" the United States and enabled it to move "towards its destiny as a global power". The 1840s doctrine of "manifest destiny", on the basis of which the US justified its expansion and renewed dispossession of Native Americans, resonates throughout the uses of memory and history at Pearl Harbor.

Visiting the Memorial

In the past two weeks I have visited Pearl Harbor twice, the first time as a tourist, participating in the performance through which a memory of the surprise attack is represented, and the second time participating in a "Not In Our Name" march on Pearl Harbor as a part of the worldwide weekend of anti-war demonstrations. Both visits took place while I was at a conference on "Cultural Diversity in a Globalising World", at which delegates from around the world grappled with theorising those key concepts, and some sought to relate their discussions to an activist consciousness.

> Pearl Harbor as 'hallowed ground' is emphasised throughout what is effectively a performance of remembering in which it is clearly anticipated that visitors will play their part.

Pearl Harbor as "hallowed ground" is emphasised throughout what is effectively a performance of remembering in which it is clearly anticipated that visitors will play their part. The performance begins upon arrival, with information boards in the grounds variously advising that "the world and

America" come to the memorial site "to mourn". Visitors are admonished to behave with "dignity" as they are on "hallowed ground". The formal performance of remembering begins with a film, followed by a boat trip out to the USS *Arizona* memorial. The performance is also a gendered one, in which a somewhat syrupy female voice narrates the film and a male voice instructs the boat passengers to and from the *Arizona* memorial in details of the Japanese attack. Thus this gendered remembering/ mourning division of labour suggests that nurturing the memory of the Japanese attack and the human cost of the war is female, whereas the site of male warrior behaviour, the battleship *Arizona* where more than a thousand men are entombed, is male. The sacredness of the *Arizona* memorial is further ensured by its spatial separation from the secular space of the visitor centre, with its theatre, memorabilia shop, toilets and ice-cream trolley.

Using signage, multimedia, and other techniques, the USS *Arizona* memorial highlights U.S. sacrifice and suffering but leaves out the United States' own history of militarism. (Getty Images.)

Past Images Resonate with Current Ones

Visitors are inducted into remembering by a uniformed official who outlines the format of the performance, including the required etiquette of behaving quietly at the *Arizona* memorial "in memory" of the crewmen who lie there. The language and euphemisms presented in the film's historical background to the Japanese attack resonate with present US obsessions and linguistic devices. Thus the Japanese seizure of Manchuria [in 1931] was carried out by "extremists", against whom the United States had to protect its "interests", and prevent the Japanese from dominating the Pacific. Oil, the audience was informed, was "the lifeblood of the Japanese war machine". That is to say, oil was in the hands of the enemy sixty years ago, as it is at present in the oilfields of Iraq (and other Middle Eastern states that may be on the US list for "liberation").

> Footage of US planes taking off from the battleships of the period dovetailed strongly with the almost daily TV news scenes of more sophisticated planes taking off from vast aircraft carriers in the Gulf.

Footage of US planes taking off from the battleships of the period dovetailed strongly with the almost daily TV news scenes of more sophisticated planes taking off from vast aircraft carriers in the Gulf. The film then cut to President [Franklin D.] Roosevelt's address to Congress and declaration of war, and a montage of battle images from various Pacific theatres of war over the next three years. In language reminiscent of what followed September 11 [2001], the attack on Pearl Harbor, the narrative continued, had "united" America. Then, miraculously it seemed, the war was over, with the film making no mention of [the U.S. atomic bombings of] Hiroshima or Nagasaki, or of the humiliating surrender forced upon the Japanese.

The *Arizona* memorial is built over the sunken remains of the battleship, which can be seen along with the
"tears of oil", the oil that continues to rise to the surface.
People stood quietly, reading the names on the com-
memorative wall, and on a smaller partial wall, names of
"survivors" of the attack who have since died. After what
apparently had been scheduled as sufficient time for "remembering", visitors were invited to return to the boat,
the trip back being punctuated by the voices of witnesses
to the attack, some of which personalised its effects, such
as one sailor wondering about two of his friends who
were on duty that day, recalling how he had hoped they
were all right, only to find that they had been killed.
Nevertheless, the main narrative voice then continued,
Americans and Japanese now meet at Pearl Harbor in
peace, "to remember", although there is no visual sign of
this apparent reconciliation.

Challenging the Meaning of the Memorial

A few days later I returned to Pearl Harbor, along with
about five hundred "Not In Our Name" protesters, including twenty-five dressed as UN weapons inspectors
complete with white zip-up contamination outfits and
pale blue helmets. Unlike sovereignty and independence
demonstrations by Indigenous Hawaiians, ours was met
with a relatively minimal and benign police and military
presence. Many of the protesters were intent on connecting Pearl Harbor's strategic importance to US control of
the Pacific with the Indigenous struggle to regain their
stolen lands. As a symbol of US domination, protesters
also highlighted that Pearl Harbor is a "chilling reminder"
to the people of Hawaii that there are plenty of weapons
of mass destruction there, whereas this has yet to be cer-
tified in Iraq. Thus one of the demands we made at the
gates of Pearl Harbor was that the authorities disclose
details of weapons kept there. The "Pledge of Resistance"

The Design of the USS *Arizona* Memorial at Pearl Harbor

President Dwight D. Eisenhower, who helped achieve Allied victory in Europe during World War II, approved the creation of the Memorial in 1958. Its construction was completed in 1961 with public funds appropriated by Congress and private donations. The Memorial was dedicated in 1962.

According to its architect, Alfred Preis, the design of the Memorial, "Wherein the structure sags in the center but stands strong and vigorous at the ends, expresses initial defeat and ultimate victory. . . . The overall effect is one of serenity. Overtones of sadness have been omitted to permit the individual to contemplate his own personal responses . . . his innermost feelings."

Contrary to popular belief, the USS *Arizona* is no longer in commission. As a special tribute to the ship and her lost crew, the United States flag flies from the flagpole, which is attached to the severed mainmast of the sunken battleship. The USS *Arizona* Memorial has come to commemorate all military personnel killed in the Pearl Harbor attack.

SOURCE. *National Park Service, USS* Arizona *Memorial, World War II: Valor in the Pacific. www.nps.gov/valr.*

that we all stood to read aloud together proclaimed our rejection of continued US militaristic behaviour to "save people from themselves", and a belief in the responsibility of people living in the US to "resist the injustices" perpetrated by the government in their name. In solidarity with others around the world who have come under attack because of their opposition to the war or for their religion or ethnicity, the pledge promised to "make real" the vision that "another world is possible".

This is a slogan that will continue to be voiced around the world, and as a slogan it is by definition simplistic. Nevertheless, behind its simplicity lie some of the answers to the angst being expressed at the Cultural Diversity conference, as the anti-war movement that is being rejuvenated—thanks to the US—represents ways in which a different kind of "globalisation" is also taking place. This is not a globalisation that homogenises and defines our destinies, but one that yet again (or still) contains the potential for unity expressed through a diversity of voices and opinions.

The Pearl Harbor Memorial Evokes Sorrow and Solidarity for Japanese Visitors

Yujin Yaguchi

Established in 1962 as a memorial to those who lost their lives in the attack on Pearl Harbor, the USS *Arizona* Memorial sees more than one million visitors each year. In the viewpoint that follows, Japanese history professor Yujin Yaguchi explores the responses of Japanese nationals who visit the memorial and finds that many of these individuals view it as a reflection of their own feelings about the war. They often express great sorrow for an act that, for many, occurred before they were born. In addition, Yaguchi reports that many Japanese citizens feel that the memorial should incorporate more information about the dropping of atomic bombs on Hiroshima and Nagasaki to encourage a greater understanding of the shared experience

---

SOURCE. Yujin Yaguchi, *The Unpredictability of the Past: Memories of the Asia-Pacific War in U.S.-East Asian Relations.* Durham, NC: Duke University Press, 2007. Copyright 2007, Duke University Press. All rights reserved. Used by permission of the publisher.

and destructive nature of war. Yujin Yaguchi has extensively researched the relationship between Japan and Hawaii since World War II.

The *Arizona* Memorial in Pearl Harbor, Hawaii, which commemorates the surprise attack on a U.S. territory by Japanese forces in 1941, is one of the most recognized landmarks in the United States. Designed by the architect Alfred Preis and built in 1960, it is dedicated to the more than one thousand men who perished on board the battleship *Arizona* on December 7, 1941. The memorial stands over the battleship, which remains sunken under the water to this day. The contrast between the bright white color of the memorial under the blue Hawaiian sky and the rusty surface of the old ship in the water generates a powerful feeling among many visitors. Located about a thirty-minute drive from Waikiki, the memorial is one of the most popular sites for tourists from the U.S. mainland who come to Hawaii, attracting nearly 1.5 million people a year. . . .

However, in a state where the economy is in significant part sustained by global tourism, visitors to the site are not limited to American nationals. In particular, every day, among the many visitors from the U.S. mainland, one can find Japanese tourists walking through the museum located at the visitors center, watching the introductory film with translation headsets, riding the Navy boat to the memorial, and gazing at the sunken battleship that was bombed by Japanese planes more than sixty years ago.

[American historian] Edward Linenthal describes how some U.S. visitors to the memorial see the presence of these Japanese as "physical defilement" of this sacred site. Complaints about the irreverent attitude of Japanese visitors are not uncommon (though very few cases are actually substantiated). Linenthal cites an incident in

Approximately 150,000 tourists from Japan visit the USS *Arizona* memorial in Pearl Harbor each year. Most express shame, sorrow, and a desire for peace. (**AP Images.**)

which an American man who mistook a group of Filipino visitors for Japanese asked the superintendent, "Why are those Japs here?" While expressions of such a negative feeling against the Japanese visitors are neither condoned nor accepted among the staff of the memorial (nothing in the visitors center and the memorial shows overt hostility to Japan or the Japanese people), this question of why the Japanese come and, more important, what the memorial means to them remains unexplored. . . .

Diversity Among Japanese Responses to the Memorial

The exact number of Japanese visitors to the *Arizona* Memorial is unknown because the Park Service does not keep a complete tally of different nationals who visit the site. A visitors survey conducted in 2000 estimates the figure to be less than 10 percent of all visitors. This would mean that about 150,000 Japanese visitors, or about 10 percent of the total who arrive in Hawaii, come to the memorial every year, a number which is in sharp contrast to the number of visitors from the mainland United States, for whom the experience is considered "a must." . . .

It must be remembered that the information used in this essay is based on a relatively select group of people: those who decided to spend some time at the memorial and after the tour were willing to share their feelings and experiences by filling out the questionnaire or in personal interviews. . . .

> Only after going through the tour did many [Japanese tourists] realize the extent of the damage the Japanese attack caused in Pearl Harbor.

Overall, the profiles of Japanese visitors to the memorial were diverse, just like the profiles of the visitors to Hawaii, which, unlike two or three decades ago, are no longer predominantly middle-class men.

The motivations for coming to the memorial seemed equally diverse. Some . . . had been influenced by the film [*Pearl Harbor*]. Older people tended to say they wanted to come because they remembered the wartime experience and wanted to see "where it all started." Some came because it was one of the stops made during the island tour. Many others, particularly those who came on their own rather than with a tour, had come simply because they had run out of places to go or wanted to do something different from shopping and sunbathing. Most of these people had been in Hawaii previously and were looking for a new experience. They had very little specific knowledge about the attack since the incident is not emphasized in Japanese history education. Only after going through the tour did many realize the extent of the damage the Japanese attack caused in Pearl Harbor and expressed great surprise to learn that so many people died on that day. . . .

A Monument to Peace

The National Park Service, which jointly operates the site with the Navy, distributes visitor survey questionnaires to those who wish to leave their impression of the memorial. The questionnaires are available in both English and Japanese and ask a series of questions with regard to visitors' impressions of the museum, film, memorial, and other aspects of the site. The questionnaire also provides a blank box where visitors are free to write their impressions or comments about the place. Over the years, a number of Japanese visitors have filled out this form and I had access to approximately four hundred completed forms.

The comments reveal a great deal about the variety of feelings the memorial triggered in the minds of these Japanese visitors. Among these, one theme that appears consistently is the visitors' desire to define the memorial as a monument dedicated to peace. There is constant use of phrases such as "War is terrible," "No more war," and "Peace is important." A seventy-six-year-old woman wrote, "War is the worst thing" and demanded that "the leaders should exercise responsibility and care for the people so that they will be able to live out their lives happily as human beings." A twelve-year-old girl wrote, "[After the tour] I felt that war is a very bad thing. It is the same as making people die." A twenty-six-year-old man noted that the "good point" about the memorial is that he was "able to realize again the tragedy and emptiness of wars as well as the reason

> The tendency of the Japanese visitors to regard the *Arizona* Memorial as a peace monument is conditioned by the fact that many war sites in Japan . . . are generally dedicated to the idea of spreading peace.

why the war happened." Finally, a sixty-two-year-old man argued, "It is important to leave this as a memorial forever so that we can confront this unfortunate incident in the past and establish an everlasting peace between the United States and Japan. I thank god that I am able to visit this place in this way at a peaceful time."

The tendency of the Japanese visitors to regard the *Arizona* Memorial as a peace monument is conditioned by the fact that many war sites in Japan, such as the museums in Hiroshima, Nagasaki, and Okinawa, are generally dedicated to the idea of spreading peace. A strong antiwar message is embedded in the narratives of such museums, as they define the Japanese citizens during World War II as tragic victims of bombings and attacks by their enemies. Japanese visitors bring this perspective when viewing the sunken battleship and find a parallel tragedy in the narrative that describes the dead sailors of the *Arizona* as hapless victims who perished on a quiet Sunday morning without fully realizing what was happening. "Even though it was an unavoidable war," wrote a fifty-year-old woman, "it is regrettable that young lives were destroyed in the water. I hope the peace will last." . . .

Integrating the Japanese Experience into the Memorial

Because the majority of the Japanese see the *Arizona* Memorial as a site dedicated to opposing wars, many expressed a strong desire to see references to Hiroshima and Nagasaki [where the U.S. dropped atomic bombs], which, in Japan, serve together as a metonymic [closely associated] symbol of peace, in the museum exhibit. . . .

A thirty-two-year-old woman wrote in a questionnaire, "I want Americans to know about Japan, about a-bombs, about the reality Japanese faced, too" because such a mutual understanding "leads to our agreement that war should never be repeated." A fifty-four-year-old schoolteacher wrote, "Our lesson to the Japanese should be 'Remember Pearl Harbor,' and to Americans it should be, 'Remember Hiroshima and Nagasaki.'" A twenty-three-year-old man captured this sentiment in another way: "You emphasize that a large number of Americans was killed. But you should also discuss Hiroshima and Nagasaki so as to show the horror of wars." . . .

> When they are confronted by the description of the Japanese attack, Japanese visitors feel intensely 'embarrassed,' 'sorry,' and 'responsible' for what happened.

Japanese visitors also consider themselves an integral part of the site because they see themselves as the descendants of the agent of the attack whose actions constitute a critical element in the making of this site. When they are confronted by the description of the Japanese attack, Japanese visitors feel intensely "embarrassed," "sorry," and "responsible" for what happened.

A man who was born a year before the attack wrote on the comment sheet, "The war was begun because the Japanese were arrogant and complacent." He continued, "As one of them, I feel sorry." A sixty-five-year-old man began, "First of all, I would like to express my sincere apology to the United States." A seventy-two-year-old woman lamented, "What a stupid thing we did, even now my heart aches." This urge to apologize is seen not only among the older generation but also among the younger generation. A twenty-eight-year-old woman wrote, "I am filled with a feeling of apology," while a fourteen year old said, "Up until now, I had a bit of grudge [against the United States] for dropping the A-bombs. But I saw this from the American perspective for the first time and realized that our ancestors did a very bad thing. I am so ashamed and want to apologize."

Thus to many Japanese the memorial itself is also theirs, even though they feel alienated and marginalized from the setting. This is a place to reflect upon the actions of their ancestors and apologize on their behalf and pray for peace in the world. A twenty-six-year-old woman visited the memorial "without thinking much about it," but "when the whole tour was over" she felt "terrible." She felt so shocked that she urged the Japanese to "think more deeply" than she did if they decide to visit the place. . . .

Japanese National Identity at the USS Arizona Memorial

Over the years, scholars have investigated various sites of national commemoration in the United States to understand and critique how such sites serve to condition the identities of visitors. Different analyses show that the significance of such memorials is often layered with complexities, as those who visit such sites see and experience the memorials differently, affected by their sex, race, class, place of birth, personal experiences, and other factors.

> The memorial produces an equally strong feeling of national identity among the Japanese visitors.

One factor that remains relatively unexplored is the visitors' citizenships and their national identities. In the United States, there is often an underlying assumption that these memorials are seen and experienced by people who identify themselves as Americans. But that is far from the case at the *Arizona* Memorial and is likely not so at any other well-known memorial either, given the current state of global tourism and the movement of people across national boundaries.

Based on interviews and questionnaires obtained during fieldwork conducted at the site, this essay has shown that the significance of the *Arizona* Memorial as a national memorial remains strong among both Japanese and American visitors. True, the Japanese sense of national belonging, which is primarily generated through their feeling of distance from the victims of the attack as well as from other visitors at the site, differs from the patriotic nationalism of the many American visitors who identify strongly with the victims. Nonetheless, the memorial produces an equally strong feeling of national identity among the Japanese visitors.

Parallels Between
Pearl Harbor and 9/11

Emily S. Rosenberg

On September 11, 2001, the people of the United States witnessed the most deadly terrorist attack ever perpetrated on
U.S. soil. Individuals belonging to the terrorist group al Qaeda
hijacked four American commercial airliners and crashed them
into the twin towers of the World Trade Center in New York City
and the Pentagon, the headquarters of the U.S. Department
of Defense, near Washington, DC. The last plane crashed into
a field in rural Pennsylvania before it could be directed to its
target—the White House. Only one incident in modern U.S. history rivals the 9/11 attacks in terms of surprise and casualties:
Pearl Harbor. In the following viewpoint, American history professor Emily S. Rosenberg examines the similarities between the
two events, focusing on the national discourse surrounding the
events in the months and years following each of the attacks.

SOURCE. Emily S. Rosenberg, "September 11, Through the Prism
of Pearl Harbor," *Chronicle of Higher Education*, vol. 50, December 5,
2003, pp. B13–14. Copyright © 2003 by the *Chronicle of Higher
Education*. This article may not be published, reposted, or redis-
tributed without express permission from the *Chronicle of Higher
Education*.

Rosenberg maintains that analyses of the similarities sheds light on U.S. foreign policy during the 1990s and 2000s and the power of metaphor in stirring public support for nationalist agendas. Emily S. Rosenberg is a professor of history at the University of California, Irvine, and the author of the book *A Date Which Will Live: Pearl Harbor and American Memory.*

The analogies came easily after September 11, 2001, when newspaper headlines picked up the cry of "Infamy!" and President [George W.] Bush reportedly wrote in his diary that "the Pearl Harbor of the 21st century took place today." As historians who focus on popular memory have insisted, we experience the present through the lens of the past—and we shape our understanding of the past through the lens of the present.

> We experience the present through the lens of the past—and we shape our understanding of the past through the lens of the present.

Pearl Harbor as an Icon of Popular Memory

During the decade of the 1990s, Pearl Harbor became an increasingly visible icon of popular memory. Although the 1941 attack had long provided a familiar metaphor with various meanings, the succession of 50th anniversaries that memorialized major World War II events helped revive interest in the symbolism of Pearl Harbor. Best sellers by [American journalist] Tom Brokaw and [American historian] Stephen E. Ambrose lauded the sacrifices of the "greatest generation" and urged Americans to honor and collect stories from aged veterans before they died.

That "memory boom" culture combined with an array of political contexts. During the economic recession of the early 1990s, a flurry of books and articles expressed often hysterical concern over U.S. weakness and the sudden economic prowess of Japan, an imbalance (in fact, short-lived) widely represented as an "economic Pearl Harbor." A movement to exonerate the military commanders at Pearl Harbor, Adm. Husband E. Kimmel and Gen. Walter C. Short, stirred controversy over who bore the blame for Pearl Harbor—the commanders in Hawaii or Franklin Roosevelt, the Democratic president in the White House. That, in turn, became part of a larger set of partisan "history wars," fought out in both politics and the media, especially after the Republican Party gained control of Congress in 1994.

Meanwhile, a new generation of Japanese American activists broke the silence of the past and asked new questions about their community's responses to that singular event that had demarcated such a sharp divide in formulations of racial and national identities. For example, an acrimonious dispute over a new memorial to Japanese American patriotism during World War II, dedicated in Washington in 2000, made public some long-simmering tensions about whether "patriotism" to American ideals consisted of complying with, or resisting, the government's ethnicity-based policies.

At the same time, a variety of strategic analysts warned of potential "Pearl Harbors" to make their case that the United States was letting down its national-security guard in the face of electronic, biological, chemical, or more conventional attacks.

Pearl Harbor, in short, became a multivocal icon that circulated with increased intensity in diverse contexts during the 1990s and beyond.

Hollywood Cements Pearl Harbor in U.S. Collective Memory

Hollywood gave the icon its biggest boost. The film *Titanic* had shown the profit-making potential of a visually stunning spectacle of disaster, love, and survival, all set in the past. The attack at Pearl Harbor, building on the popularity of the "greatest generation" phenomenon, seemed a near-perfect vehicle for a similar blockbuster. Made with assistance from the Pentagon, *Pearl Harbor* was extravagant in every way: costs ($135 million), spectacle (merging the actual explosion of old warships with new computer-generated graphics), and promotion. The movie premiered just before Memorial Day 2001, amid a shower of associated television specials, magazine covers, books, consumer offshoots, and journalistic promotions. As it turned out, the film flopped in the reviews and then disappointed expectations at the box office and in DVD sales.

By the summer of 2001, nevertheless, memories of Pearl Harbor—now circulating within a generation that had no direct recollection of the attack—had become so ubiquitous in American culture that a stranger to the planet might have imagined that the attack had just recently occurred. Less than four months after the premiere of *Pearl Harbor*, after a summer and spring of hype, those refreshed and updated memories would shape the reactions to a new, even more deadly, surprise attack.

> Structured by the Pearl Harbor story, September 11 seemed the prelude to another struggle between good and evil.

Pearl Harbor Comparisons Ease National Anxiety

"Infamy" framed the first representations of September 11. That word, which since 1941 had become a virtual synonym for the Pearl Harbor attack, was culturally legible to almost everyone. It invoked a familiar, even comforting, narrative: a sleeping nation, a treacherous attack, and the need to rally patriotism and "manly" virtues on behalf of retribution. Structured by the Pearl Harbor story, September 11 seemed the prelude to another struggle between good and evil; to the testing of yet another "greatest generation"; and to an inevitable, righteous victory. The [George W.] Bush administration and other politicians embraced that Pearl Harbor metaphor as they prepared to strike the Taliban in Afghanistan, and journalists seemed unable to resist reacting to Al Qaeda's assaults within the rhetorical conventions of Pearl Harbor. It was a ready, and easy, metaphor. Experts who flooded the airwaves more often addressed World War II parallels than the complexities of, say, Middle Eastern politics.

The familiar melodramatic structure—deadly threat followed by resolve and unconditional military triumph—helped sketch a powerfully reassuring story about a world that, for Americans, was suddenly filled with mourning, national insecurity, and personal anxiety. The symbol of Pearl Harbor offered a healing balm in a time of great popular fear and keep-the-message-simple mass media.

Less than three months after the fall of the towers, the 60th-anniversary commemorations of the Pearl Harbor attack itself further solidified the identification between the two events. New Yorkers journeyed to Hawaii to embrace Pearl Harbor survivors. [Former president] George H.W. Bush addressed both attacks in speeches at two museums that honored the Pacific War. His son, the president, proclaimed Dec. 7 National Pearl Harbor Remembrance Day, with a reminder about "the presence of evil in the world"; then he flew to Norfolk, Va., to gather with people who had witnessed the Pearl Harbor attack. From the deck of one of the first aircraft carriers to launch strikes against the Taliban in Afghanistan, he proclaimed, "We've seen their kind before. The terrorists are the heirs to fascism." Once Pearl Harbor and September 11 became rhetorically intertwined, however, the spread of disparate meanings could not be easily contained. The attack on Pearl Harbor had never represented only one story, one "lesson," or one set of rhetorical conven-

In the months after the terrorist attacks on September 11, 2001, U.S. president George W. Bush used the history of Pearl Harbor to suggest that the two events were analogous. (**AP Images.**)

tions. If the framework of "infamy" initially marshaled remembrance of a deadly surprise attack by "evil" racial others, the story of Pearl Harbor could easily evoke other contexts as well.

The Sleeping Metaphor Reemerges

One of those was the "sleeping" metaphor. American films, cartoons, comedians, and commentators during World War II commonly depicted "Uncle Sam" as having been "asleep" during the 1930s. One of the most widely read books on Pearl Harbor after the war was [American historian] Gordon W. Prange's *At Dawn We Slept*, and nearly every rendition of the attack since the [1971] film *Tora! Tora! Tora!* has invoked the quote, attributed to the Japanese admiral Isoroku Yamamoto, about the dangers of "awakening a sleeping giant."

During World War II, the sleeping metaphor was often directed at isolationists, specifically at Roosevelt's Republican opponents in Congress, who had resisted any substantial military buildup during the 1930s. Now it helped frame questions about America's preparedness for the attacks of September 11, but this time it had been Congress and its panels of expert witnesses who had warned publicly of future "Pearl Harbors" and urged greater alertness. *Time* magazine's cover of May 27, 2002, featured "WHILE AMERICA SLEPT" in big red letters. Underneath were the statements "What Bush Knew Before 9/11" and "Why So Little Was Done." This year [2003, American investigative journalist] Gerald L. Posner's detailed study of intelligence and other political failures leading up to the September 2001 attacks took the title *Why America Slept*.

Americans Again Search for Someone to Blame

Questions about blame also suggested another Pearl Harbor-era word: "Inquiry." There had been numerous wartime and postwar investigations of what went wrong at Pearl Harbor. At the time, it was Republicans who charged the Roosevelt administration and the Democratic-controlled Congress with trying to protect themselves by scapegoating the commanders in Hawaii. Having gained control of Congress in 1994, Republicans, along with a few Democratic allies, called for new investigations into Pearl Harbor and shifted the blame for the lack of preparedness to President Franklin Roosevelt.

By 2003, however, the politics of inquiry were very different.

A Republican president confronted questions about his administration's failure to anticipate a surprise attack, and a Republican Congress rallied to limit investigations. Finally forced to appoint an independent, bipartisan investigation, the Bush administration and the commission locked horns over access to documents, just as had happened during the Pearl Harbor investigations more than 50 years earlier. As Republican enthusiasm for new inquiries into Pearl Harbor faded, Democratic calls for ones related to September 11 mounted. As the Republican Bush administration built an enlarged national security state, it crafted, ironically, new governmental powers and claims of secrecy that were reminiscent of the Democratic Roosevelt's wartime administration.

The Back Door to War Becomes the Back Door to Empire

Slowly but steadily, yet another Pearl Harbor analogy emerged. Just after December 7, Roosevelt's most embittered critics charged him with manipulating a "back door to war"—provoking a Japanese attack and opening a "back door" to American involvement in the war that had already engulfed Europe. The more extreme view suggested a dark conspiracy: The Roosevelt administration knew the attack was coming, failed to send clear and urgent messages of an imminent assault to the Pacific commanders, and then covered up its misdeeds. A milder version argued simply that Roosevelt welcomed a convenient provocation to enter the war and did nothing to avoid its coming. Those back-door stories, which had circulated throughout the postwar era, gained additional visibility during the 1990s.

In an analysis of the Bush administration's policy making published in 2002, the always provocative [American author] Gore Vidal overtly invoked the title of one of the most prominent back-door works, *Perpetual War for Perpetual Peace*, edited by Harry Elmer Barnes in 1953. In his own back-door-to-empire interpretation, Vidal postulated that the Bush-Cheney oil group had plotted to beef up America's imperial presence in the Caspian and gulf oil regions and then used Al Qaeda's conveniently timed attack to justify conquest.

Michael Meacher, a former minister in [British prime minister] Tony Blair's government, writing in *The Guardian* pointed to the pre-9/11 imperial dreams of the Project for the New American Century, a private group that included people who subsequently became top members of the Bush defense establishment. A report by the group, Meacher wrote, had even argued that it would take some new "Pearl Harbor" to get Americans to support their globalist agenda, and he implied that some kind of attack would not have been entirely unwelcome. Back-door-to-empire interpretations, very prevalent outside of the United States, increasingly gained visibility here at home as questions began to circulate about ignored intelligence briefings, the Federal Aviation Administration's decisions on September 11, and puzzling timetables about what the president was told and when he was told it.

> Pearl Harbor and September 11 thus stand as reusable and interrelated icons, shaping popular memories of the past and present.

History Offers an Arena for Debate

Politicians, in particular, often claim that the study of history teaches certain clear, and singular, "lessons." An examination of the uses of Pearl Harbor, however, suggests that history offers an arena for a diversity of narratives and for continuing debate about their possible meanings. Pearl Harbor stories have long been generating diverse debates, especially over the conduct of foreign policy, the global expansion of American power, and executive-branch responsibility. It is hardly surprising that September 11, so embedded within Pearl Harbor's metaphorical structures, has already sparked controversy over similar concerns. The politics of memory are no less complex than any other form of politics.

Pearl Harbor and September 11 thus stand as reusable and interrelated icons, shaping popular memories of past and present. Through Pearl Harbor, many of the rhetorical conventions of September 11 have been established; through September 11, the diverse understandings of Pearl Harbor have been reiterated. Through both events, longstanding debates about government's role and the direction of foreign policy can be refracted, recalled, and conducted anew.

CHAPTER 3

Personal Narratives

DORIE MILLER
*Received the Navy Cross
at Pearl Harbor, May 27, 1942*

A Veteran Describes the Attack on Pearl Harbor and Its Aftermath

L.E. Rogers

Photo on previous page: An Office of War Information poster commemorates naval mess attendant Dorie Miller, who was stationed on the USS *West Virginia* and shot down four enemy aircrafts. (**Getty Images.**)

Al Rogers was a twenty-one-year-old aviation machinist's mate assigned to Pearl Harbor's Kaneohe Naval Air Station when the Japanese attack came. In the following viewpoint, Rogers' son, L.E. Rogers, gives his father's account of the incoming Japanese aircraft and the bombing of the field and the hangars where the U.S. defense planes were stationed. In a dramatic retelling, Rogers captures the surprise of the attack and the devastation wrought upon the airfield, as well as the bewilderment that followed. Following Pearl Harbor, Al Rogers served throughout the Pacific and attained the rank of petty officer first class.

SOURCE. L.E. Rogers, "Duel in the Rising Sun: A Young Aviation Machinist's Mate and a Veteran Japanese Zero Pilot Squared Off at Pearl Harbor. Only One Would Survive," *Aviation History*, January 2010, pp. 32–37. Reproduced by permission.

The date December 7, 1941, had been etched in my father's memory, as it had for so many of his generation. Decades later, in his 50s, his gray hair crew cut and with the sinewy build of an ironworker, he sat at the kitchen table, a grain belt beer held in rough, calloused hands. "Well," he'd begin in a halting, self-conscious manner, and his account would play out.

Remembering Pearl Harbor

Quincy Street Northeast, Minneapolis, had been home, the Hawaiian Islands merely pictures in a *National Geographic* magazine. In the late 1930s, Al Rogers left family behind to labor with the Civilian Conservation Corps, then set out to join the U.S. Navy. On Thanksgiving Day 1941, Navy patrol flying boats lined the seaplane ramps at Kaneohe Bay on the northeast side of Oahu. Rogers, a 21-year-old aviation machinist's mate, was assigned to Patrol Squadron 12 at the naval air station.

By November 26, the Japanese Combined Fleet had begun its long voyage through restless Pacific waters, a journey that was predestined to intertwine the fates of my father and a Japanese naval fighter pilot. Aboard the aircraft carrier *Soryu*, Lieutenant Fusata Iida, a rising star in the Imperial Japanese Navy, wondered what lay ahead. A graduate of the Eta Jima Military School, honored with the Imperial Prize, and an aggressive pilot who had honed his skills over China, Iida would soon add to his stature in the sky above Oahu.

Two hundred twenty miles north of Hawaii at 6 A.M. on Sunday, December 7, the first wave of aircraft lifted off from Japanese carrier decks. As the planes droned through the scattered clouds of a rising Pacific sun, Oahu slept on, unsuspecting. In the naval air station barracks at Kaneohe Bay, the usual morning chatter and noise grew exceptionally loud at about 7:50 A.M. Tired and irritable after working through the night, Al Rogers, a scrappy lightweight, rolled out of his bunk, tightened a fist and started after the loudest sailor in the bunch. Suddenly the roar of radial-engine aircraft overhead drowned out the sailors' babble, and he heard chaotic shouts:

"What the hell . . . ?

"Must be Army maneuvers."

"Those big red circles . . ."

Machine guns began to hammer away. One sailor pointed out the window and yelled, "It's Jap planes!"

The barracks shuddered. A Zero [carrier-based fighter plane] careened by, tracers from its gun ports streaking toward the administration building. Amid the confusion, Rogers frantically donned dress white trousers, a blue work shirt, boots and a white sailor's cap—the mix of uniform irrelevant.

The Attack Begins

Kaneohe was under attack!

Japanese planes hurtled down at the air station, a murderous swarm of fighters and bombers. Explosions and gunfire filled the air. Near Hangar One a half dozen Consolidated PBY-5 Catalina flying boats [a type of seaplane] were engulfed in flames. Armor-piercing rounds ripped through their hulls. Fuel tanks exploded into vast columns of fire and smoke. Resolute sailors and Marines struck back in vain, armed only with rifles, light machine guns and even pistols. Some of them paid with their lives.

As suddenly as they arrived, the invaders departed—dark, deadly specs droning into the eastern sky. Kaneohe's PBYs, scouts of the Pacific Fleet, burned in the early dawn.

Rogers made his way through the disaster scene until he reached his assigned plane outside Hangar One. Close by, PBYs blazed and fires sent monstrous clouds of black, acrid smoke billowing into the blue Pacific sky.

At his duty station, the skipper's PBY, Rogers climbed inside the hull, feeling ill at ease among the more experienced hands already there. In each of the open waist ports, .50-caliber machine guns sat in their mounts. Extra cans of ammo hung on the bulkhead amidships, and a .30-caliber stood ready in the bow turret.

"I don't think they'll be back," said one sailor with angry bravado.

"After all," said another, "we're ready for 'em now."

Amid the crackling fires and black smoke, the burning aluminum flying boats melted to the ground. The men inside the skipper's plane anxiously manned their stations and seethed for revenge, trying to comprehend the calamity. Finally some went after additional ammo, a couple more to search for coffee. One of them remarked, "This is going to be a long day."

Rogers remained in the plane with the radioman, a member of the regular flight crew. They watched the sky as the PBYs burned.

The Second Wave

It was about 9 A.M. when sailors in Hangar One suddenly pointed to the sky. A second wave of nine Japanese fighters, led by Lieutenant Iida, was storming in from the north, intent on finishing the job that the first wave had started.

As the radioman started forward through the fuselage, he yelled back to Rogers: "They're coming back! You take the .50s, I'll take the .30 in the bow."

Rogers, an airframe mechanic, not a gunner, called the radioman back. Quickly, the man explained: "This is the trigger. This is the charging handle, and this is practice ammo. Every tenth round is a dud."

Incredulous, Rogers exclaimed, "Duds!"

"Don't worry," urged the radioman. "Just pull the handle back, and it's ready to go again." With that he turned and hurried forward, gunnery 101 concluded.

The enemy planes descended upon the air station while Rogers mentally reviewed the instructions for firing the .50-caliber. As the formation drew closer, he fired

one quick burst, and die rounds fell short of the lead plane.

The Zeros, in single file, circled the air station, death and destruction in their wake. Again they returned toward the flight line and hangars, firing both guns and cannons. Rogers lined up his gun, bullets arcing behind his targets. At every tenth round, his tension mounted with each maddening pull of the charging handle. The clattering of the .50 resounded within the PBY's hull as if it were a 55-gallon drum. Shell casings tumbled to the deck.

"Like shooting pheasants, lead the target," Rogers mumbled to himself. "Lead the goddamn target!"

The carnage continued as Japanese guns mauled the blazing hulks of the venerable flying boats. Graceful and slow in flight, on the ground the PBY-5s sat like marooned whales, perched on their beaching gear, large dual wheels to the port and starboard sides, a tail wheel affixed to the stern. Sailors scattered for cover amid the belching fires and smoke, the constant roar of Japanese airplanes, the rattle of machine guns.

Angry and shaken, Rogers realigned his short bursts, catching another train of incoming fighters. The planes headed toward the barracks, shops, armory and administration buildings, strafing as they went. Out over the bay a lone A6M2 Zero circled, then swooped down.

Downing the Lead Japanese Fighter Plane

Like a winged samurai, Fusata Iida banked his Zero and hurtled down through the smoke and fire. Sweat-soaked, heart pounding and angry as hell, Rogers held his fire. He was determined not to miss this time around.

The fighter pilot, seemingly intent on eliminating the troublesome gunners in the skipper's plane, closed on his target. A flutter of smoke curled behind the Zero's wings, as nose and wing guns blazed. At the last moment—"lead

Photo on previous pages: Japanese military planes could be recognized by the red circles on their wings and bodies. (Check Six.)

the goddamn target"—Rogers fired one short burst, stitching the Zero. Iida abruptly banked away, roaring over 1st Street. Groundfire erupted from the armory.

Moments later, Iida's flight formed up and turned for Gun Sight Pass, a gap in the mountains across Kaneohe Bay. But Iida himself lagged behind the formation, which flew to his side. Below, Rogers and the radioman watched and waited.

Lieutenant junior grade Iyozo Fujita immediately assessed the problem: Iida's plane was trailing fuel. The Japanese flight leader had been hit by groundfire. Iida pointed at himself, then at the ground. Fujita remembered his friend's prophetic affirmation that morning on *Soryu*. In the event he could not complete his mission, Iida had said, "I will crash dive into an enemy target rather than attempt an emergency landing." Iida waved his men off and dived toward the bay. Fujita watched helplessly as his comrade plummeted toward Kaneohe.

Iida's Zero plunged toward the water and leveled off, the angle of dive and recovery abrupt. Engine screaming, the A6M2 swept toward the seaplane ramps and Hangar One.

In the hope of luring his adversary closer, Rogers stepped away from his gun and tugged at the auxiliary ammunition rack on the bulkhead of the PBY. The Zero howled across the ramps, its gunfire chewing through the smoldering seaplanes. At the last minute, Rogers lunged back into position, grabbed the .50-caliber and aimed at Iida's Zero. A vapor trail streamed from the plane; its cannons blew chunks of debris from the flight line, ever nearer to the PBY.

Iida roared closer, making no attempt to alter his angle of attack. Rogers fired the .50-caliber, and a plume of smoke and lick of flame streamed from the engine. The Zero was hit!

Undaunted, Iida careened over 1st Street toward the armory. Aviation Ordnanceman Sands opened up with automatic rifle fire as the plane plowed into the ground, its airframe buckling on impact. The huge radial engine, torn from its mounts, cartwheeled to rest at the side of a house. Fusata Iida crushed within the wreckage.

The radioman clambered back through the fuselage from the bow turret of the PBY. Rogers, elated, yelled, "We got one!"

"What do you mean, we?" said the radioman. "You got 'em yourself! Our wing was in the way. I couldn't shoot." (In the disorder that permeates the heat of battle, several servicemen would lay claim to having shot down Iida, but my father never wavered in his memory of the day's events.)

> On December 8, the air station smoldered in the still dawn.

Their exuberance was short-lived. Behind them Hangar One exploded when a bomb plunged through its roof. Debris rained across the flight line; fires and clouds of acrid smoke blotted out the sky.

In the commotion, Rogers and the radioman rushed toward the inferno. A burned sailor with a broken leg dragged himself from the wreckage. In the heat and smoke, they pulled the man to safety, putting him in a passing truck with other wounded. The nameless radioman rode along to help.

Alone, Rogers climbed back into the PBY, assessing the damage. Blistered paint, burnt flaps, shrapnel through the hull, flat tires—it wouldn't fly soon. Rogers was still incensed, but like the skipper's plane, he too was spent. After a long while, both he and his guns were commandeered, carted off to the hilltop in the middle of the air station.

After the Attack on Pearl Harbor

An edgy vigil ensued. Through the long night that followed, the occasional boom of howitzers echoed from the hills across the bay and tracers sliced through the murky darkness. As rumors circulated, the besieged sailors strained their eyes, searching for an invasion that never came. Over the Koolau Range, Pearl Harbor, afire, glowed in the night sky.

On December 8, the air station smoldered in the still dawn. Twenty-seven PBYs had been transformed into charred hulks. The hangars were a tangle of rubble, blackened by fire and smoke; the dead were still being counted.

Relieved from their gun post, Rogers and a fellow sailor trudged by the station infirmary toward what remained of their barracks.

"Hey, sailors, over here," came a commanding voice from behind.

The station doctor had hailed them. In a bloodied uniform and with a haggard, determined expression on his face, he was a man not to be trifled with. Both sailors were taken to the infirmary garage, which was serving as a makeshift morgue, and given hammers and nails to make coffins.

> Thoughts of dead and wounded soldiers, the embattled air station and being machine-gunned by the man who lay before him raced through Rogers' mind.

"Get busy," said the doctor. "I'll find more help."

Four more sailors soon arrived. The "Doc" sent another six to the barracks to dress for a burial detail.

As the sailors prepared coffins, two Marines arrived in a jeep. They unloaded a trash can and placed it next to the infirmary entrance. Slumped inside the container were the remains of the only Japanese pilot shot down at Kaneohe. The can sat near the door for much of the day, until the sailors finished preparations for their fallen mates. Clad in a bloody flight suit, the body in the trash can was finally brought in. Battered and broken, Fusata Iida was laid out on a wood table.

Honoring Fallen Comrades

Thoughts of dead and wounded sailors, the embattled air station and being machine-gunned by the man who lay before him raced through Rogers' mind. Anger, weariness and grim bewilderment displaced any feelings he might have had for his fallen adversary. Tall for a Jap, he thought, then hammered nails into the pine box for the man he and others had shot from the sky.

Later that day, an honor guard of sailors and Marines trucked 16 pine coffins to a secluded gully beside the sea. At the same site, the remains of Lieutenant Iida were lowered into a separate grave.

Anonymous, Al Rogers stood quietly on a sand hill in the back row of the farewell formation, still wearing his white trousers, hat and blue work shirt. A cadre of helmeted Marines in khaki with rifles and sailors in dress whites stood at attention. All hands turned to. Over hard-faced salutes, gun salvos echoed across the ravine. The mournful wail of Taps faded into the wind and rolling surf. For the men in coffins, the day of infamy in the rising sun had ended—but for the survivors the terrible war in the Pacific had just begun.

> For the men in coffins, the day of infamy in the rising sun had ended—but for the survivors the terrible war in the Pacific had just begun.

Following Pearl Harbor, my father served throughout the Pacific in patrol squadron VP-12. During the liberation of the Philippines, he was assigned to the air division of the light cruiser *Denver* (CL-58). He attained the rank of petty officer first class. After the war he returned to Minneapolis and raised his family. He died in March 1979 as the sun rose over the Horse Heaven Hills of Washington State, another member of the "Greatest Generation" gone west.

A Japanese American Recounts the Impact of Pearl Harbor on His Parents

Charles Shiro Inouye

In the following viewpoint, Charles Shiro Inouye recounts the aftermath of the attack on Pearl Harbor on his parents, Japanese Americans who were sent to live in a relocation camp in Wyoming. Even though his parents were both citizens of the United States, they were plucked from their homes and sent to live in an internment camp. Forty-six years later, President Ronald Regan signed HR 442, a bill to redress the wartime internment of Japanese American civilians. Inouye discusses the importance of the bill, not because of its financial reparations but because of its apologetic nature. Through understanding past mistakes, Inouye contends, democracy is strengthened.

SOURCE. Charles Shiro Inouye, "I Remember Pearl Harbor: Dealing with the 'Problem Race.' (HR 442 as an Affirmation of U.S. Civil Rights)," The *Nation*, vol. 272.18, December 12, 1988, pp. 641–643. Reproduced by permission.

Franklin D. Roosevelt called the Japanese attack on Pearl Harbor forty-seven years ago "a day that will live in infamy," but infamy is hard to gauge. We are a nation of many peoples, and international insult is not always uniformly felt. December 7, 1941, was a fateful day for my own family. But perhaps more infamous was February 19, 1942, when President Roosevelt, a man who had posed as the immigrant's friend and as a leader with a vision of a fairer America, signed Executive Order 9066. That order eventually set apart Washington, Oregon, the western half of California and the southern third of Arizona as areas from which all persons of Japanese ancestry were to be removed. That included my father, who was living in Menlo Park, California, and my mother, who was living in Yakima, Washington. They were sent to live in a relocation camp in Wyoming.

The Impact of Pearl Harbor for Japanese Americans

They were both citizens of the United States and thus guaranteed certain rights by the Constitution. Their right to address the decision that would uproot them from their homes, for example, was actually honored by the creation of a forum in which all Japanese-Americans were invited to participate. These were the so-called Tolan hearings, headed by Representative John Tolan of California. This public debate on the evacuation question began on February 21, 1942, and ended on March 12. The 980-page report of the hearings eloquently describes a travesty. Set against the testimony of the military experts and those of other proevacuation groups (who for three decades had found a voice in the newspapers of William Randolph Hearst), the voice of my grandfather's people is weak and pitiful.

The issei, or first generation immigrants, not only spoke English poorly but also, having lived in segregated farming and fishing communities, had little experience as debaters. Their children, the nisei, had attended public schools and frequently became valedictorians and salutatorians in their pursuit of the American dream; but they were simply too young to protect themselves in such a hostile arena. What the decision-making process that led to the evacuation tells us is that an offer to participate in the democratic process does not necessarily ensure justice. Invited to dine at the fox's home, the heron ate poorly.

This is not to say that the forum made no difference. It did. Study the arguments of those who were in favor of the evacuation and you will find an interesting shift in strategy.

At first, the crux of this modest proposal to remove tens of thousands of ethnic Japanese from their homes and put them in concentration camps built in the outback of America was that the non-Japanese on the West Coast must be protected from invasion. The Army claimed that the Japanese immigrants were signaling submarines off the coast, secretly participating in other deeds of sabotage and, therefore, had to be sent somewhere else. (My mother, for instance, who had taken a job as a live-in maid for a dentist in Seattle, was interrogated by the Federal Bureau of Investigation because her bedroom window overlooked Puget Sound.) Though many such accusations were made, none were substantiated. Later, retreating from their obviously racist position, proponents of evacuation formed an argument that was at least outwardly more benign: The government of the United States must act quickly in order to protect Japanese immigrants from the whites who were seeking to harm them.

An Insidious Form of Inequality

Now things were switched around—the mouse was chasing the cat. But whatever the case, this burden of protection that the military took upon itself (despite objections from the Justice Department) presupposed an insidious form of inequality. As the history of blacks and Native Americans in the United States also demonstrates, governmental protection is, for all its comforting rhetoric, too often a denial of justice and dignity. It requires restrictions of liberty and asks that the "problem race" be grateful for the many favors extended to it. Those favors would in the case of the Japanese include, to quote the stone and brass historical marker that graces what remains of the Heart Mountain camp in Wyoming, "first-class schools, electricity and plumbing."

Last summer, forty-six years after the fact, President Reagan signed HR 442, a bill to redress the wartime internment of Japanese-American civilians. This acknowledges the injustice of Roosevelt's act and stands as a national apology and as a tax break to those evacuees still alive. I separate the apology from the stipend because that is how the survivors of the evacuation see it. What does $20,000, to be paid over a ten-year period, mean to people who were forced from their homes by hysterical overreaction? The money is a pittance, one my parents never expected to receive and one that will give them little joy. (There is talk about pooling the money to establish scholarship funds for the needy, and to create research grants for the study of Japanese-American history.)

But the apology really matters. The bill may be essentially an attempt at restitution, but it should not be understood as something designed to restore dignity to the JapaneseAmericans. While it is undeniable that the nisei have been fighting to regain face ever since Roosevelt's order, in truth they never lost their self-respect. Along with one suitcase of personal effects, dignity was some

> What does $20,000, to be paid over a ten-year period, mean to people who were forced from their homes by hysterical overreaction?

Photo on opposite page: The U.S. government relocated thousands of people of Japanese descent because it feared they might become involved in sabotage. (Getty Images.)

thing everyone took with them to the camps. The evacuation did not disgrace those who went but those who sent them.

The point is that if patriotism and the Pledge of Allegiance can be revived as unifying national concerns, as George [H.W.] Bush deployed them in the recent campaign, then so must dignity and the ability to apologize for our mistakes. This is why HR 442 is an important milestone in our journey as a nation. By seeing that justice is done, HR 442 restores our commitment to the belief that all people deserve to be treated well. As an affirmation of civil rights, this act makes all Americans a bit more humane because it admits that we as a group can make mistakes, that we can be contrite and that we can do something about our errors. Finally, the bill is important because it raises the issue of a national apology and brings into focus the relationship of the individual to the state in a way that no amount of flag-waving can.

As brilliant as fireworks may be, we can only see ourselves clearly in light that is more focused and steady. Too bad, then, that for every well-developed thought about the real state of our union there are a hundred empty slogans and a million statements of self-congratulation. Rare are the moments when nations are forced to think about themselves in something other than a celebratory or a defensive way. Japan's unconditional surrender to the Allied forces was, to bring in a relevant point of comparison, one of these rare moments. As Emperor Hirohito spoke to his people, he renounced his own divinity; and by this act the symbols and institutions that had brought a nation together to wage war suddenly lost authority. This was precisely what the United States sought. Our country, the victor, saw state Shinto [ancient Japanese spiritual traditions] as an abomination; and, after dropping nuclear bombs on two of Japan's cities, we forced a spiritual apology in order to plant the seeds of pluralism in the scorched wasteland of the Japanese soul.

Japanese Regret

What most Americans fail to realize is that the vast majority of Japanese actually do regret having fought the war. They regret it more profoundly than we, who, ironically, are now asking them to remilitarize. Led by the belief that they were a chosen and blessed nation, they engaged in a program of destruction and bloodshed that left much of East Asia in ashes. It was a hellish experience; and the remorse felt by some segments of the population is still so intense that the museums erected to the memory of Hiroshima and Nagasaki have been carefully denuded of any sign of politics, lest they become rallying points for partisans who would interfere with the orderly building of the new and improved Japan.

Consequently, the message we get as we walk past the photographs of melted buildings and torn flesh in the Hiroshima display is that science has created a terrible device, and that the device, not the people who design and use it, is evil. What do human beings have to do with nuclear destruction at all? In the museum display, there are, after all, no people except bombed people. Americans are not blamed. Not even Japan's wartime leaders are implicated by the jars of pickled tumors; and this possibly because the evil of mass murder is better understood on their side of the Pacific than it has ever been in this country. Japan's present silence on Hiroshima is the supreme understatement of our time. Only an American would think that silence means nothing.

Though the Japanese sense of national apology is complex and at times difficult to understand, one thing we can probably say is that it is profound in comparison to ours. By winning the "Good War" we lost much goodness, even though our false sense of righteousness blinds us to the loss. Self-congratulation has helped to erase our memories of atrocity. To our way of thinking, the atrocities simply did not exist. Why else would the radio commentator Paul Harvey declare that God gave us the first nuclear weapon because no other nation on earth was righteous enough to use it correctly? One can't help but wonder if Harvey's God is also the one inserted into the Pledge of Allegiance after the war, when "one nation, with liberty and justice for all" became "one nation, under God, with liberty and justice for all."

> If we as a democratic people have anything to congratulate ourselves about, it is not our ability to obliterate Hiroshima and Nagasaki but our power to pass a bill that redresses a national mistake, that makes us a bit nobler because of its apology.

The addition to the original Pledge of Allegiance, some will say, is an improvement because it clarifies the divine nature of our state and the very point of our unity. Having made the Japanese renounce their divinity, we apparently feel a bit more upbeat about ours. But if we are united by this godliness and even made free and just by it (as the Pledge can be interpreted), then we must be free enough and righteous enough to ask the overwhelming question: Who sent the Japanese-Americans to the wasteland?

Even God has only one vote in a democracy such as ours. Our mistakes should be recognized as our own, and so must our regrets and apologies. The decision to evacuate the Japanese from the West Coast and southern Arizona was made by people—not by evanescent powers such as those lurking behind passive-voiced Reaganisms like "mistakes were made." If we as a democratic people have anything to congratulate ourselves about, it is not our ability to obliterate Hiroshima and Nagasaki but our power to pass a bill that redresses a national mistake, that makes us a bit nobler because of its apology.

A Young Seaman Recounts the Sinking of the USS *Arizona*

Martin Matthews

Seaman Martin Matthews was 15 years old when he visited his Navy buddy William Stafford aboard the USS *Arizona* on the night of December 6, 1941. When the dawn came, Matthews and many of the crew of the battleship were rocked below decks by the explosions of Japanese bombs that targeted the capital ships in the harbor. Matthews, a visitor and a very scared young boy, did not know what was happening and had no station to man when the ship sounded general quarters. In the following viewpoint, Matthews recounts thirty years later how he survived the attack and witnessed the destruction of the *Arizona*, which exploded and sank, by falling overboard and clinging to a buoy in the harbor. His friend, Seaman Williams, perished at his post, one of the 1,177 crewmen of the *Arizona* that were killed that day.

SOURCE. Martin Matthews, *Remembering Pearl Harbor: Eyewitness Accounts by U.S. Military Men and Women*. Wilmington, DE: Scholarly Resources, 1991. Copyright © 1991 by Scholarly Resources, Inc. All rights reserved. Reproduced by permission.

W e went aboard that night [December 6, 1941]. There was a different officer of the day aboard, but word had been left that [Seaman First Class William] Stafford was bringing a friend. He asked if I might spend the night, and the O.D. said, "There's no reason for him not to." I showed him my pass from the naval air station, and I spent the night there.

Stafford's quarters were on the aft [toward the rear] part of the ship, the boat deck or the boat well. I slept in a bunk in his compartment. We went to sleep because we were tired, and we got up fairly early the next morning about 6:00. I got up earlier than usual because of the excitement of being aboard a battleship.

Sunday breakfast started at 6:00. We were wearing dress whites because we were going to do some sightseeing. We finished chow about 6:30, and we spent the next twenty minutes or so on a tour of the ship. Then we were back on the aft boat well about 7:15 or 7:30. It's hard to remember the exact time, but it was approximately that.

> We didn't know what a bomb was yet; I had never seen one in my life.

We were just talking in generalities, and I told him how much I enjoyed it and that I was looking forward to coming back aboard ship. I even said: "I wish I could get duty aboard a battleship," not knowing any better at the time. We were going to go ashore again and spend some more liberty, since I didn't have to be back to Ford Island until approximately 10:00 that night.

But then we heard noise over to our starboard [right] side. You could see a bunch of planes coming in, but nobody paid any attention to them. Then you could hear what seemed like thundering in the background, which actually were bombs starting to drop, but none of us thought about bombs. We didn't know what a bomb was yet; I had never seen one in my life.

Something Was Wrong

But as the planes got closer, the thunder got closer, and then we started seeing clouds of smoke coming up from across the roads there, the roads or channels that the ships went in and out on. Then we saw fire and explosions where the bombs hit. Well, we knew that something was wrong, but we thought that maybe it was gunnery practice.

We didn't know that the Japanese were actually attacking us; it wasn't until after the first wave went across that we knew. No bombs hit the *Arizona* during that first attack that I remember, but there was one bomb that hit a destroyer off of Ford Island. I didn't know at the time, but I found out later that it was the *Shaw*. In fact, it broke her in half.[1] Then I think that's when General Quarters was sounded on the *Arizona*.

Stafford said: "I've got to go! I'll see you later!" I remember those words. I had no place to go; I didn't even know what General Quarters was. So I just stayed in the back part of the ship. Pandemonium broke loose; sailors were running everywhere. It was a state of confusion. Guns had been encased and not prepared at all for a possible battle; they were having difficulty uncovering them; many of the guns were plugged.

We hadn't been hit yet as I remember. It could have been because there were a lot of explosions going on, but I don't remember it. It was fifteen or twenty minutes after that, which, if I remember right, would be in the neighborhood of 8:30, that she evidently was hit with a torpedo. I didn't know what a torpedo was, either, but I heard a thunderous explosion, and fire went up on the starboard side.

It shook me; it shuddered the ship, but it didn't knock me over. I can remember several incidents, particularly on the aft battery there. The antiaircraft guns, which then, I remember, were 50-calibers—they didn't have the modern version—and I could see the gunners trying to get ammunition from the ammunition locker.

Confusion in the Ranks

The boatswain's mate in charge of the ammunition locker, even with all the bombing and strafing and planes overhead—it was obvious we were being attacked at this point—refused to release ammunition from the gun locker without the permission of the officer of the day. Of course, nobody knew where the hell the officer of the day was.

Finally, one boatswain's mate, who was in charge of one gun crew, I remember well, told this chief, if he didn't get his ass out of the way, he was going to knock it out of the way. So he proceeded to do the same and hit this chief and knocked him out of the way and then broke the lock on the ammunition locker and took the ammunition from it to feed the guns to do some shooting. He used a marlinespike to break in.

> I think the second bomb that hit [the USS *Arizona*] was close to the aft deck that I was on, and, needless to say, I was petrified.

But shortly after that is when it got thick and heavy. The first bomb or two hit the *Arizona*. I think the second bomb that hit was close to the aft deck that I was on, and, needless to say, I was petrified. To put it in plain English, it scared the living hell out of me. The concussion from it did knock me down a couple of times, but my adrenalin was pumping about a thousand miles an hour, and sweat broke out all over me. I wasn't experienced with war; I hadn't been trained for it.

I was trying to get under cover, but at my age and not prepared for this, I was scared to death. This was not what I went into the Navy for, and it was not what I wanted. Besides I had no place to go. I didn't have a General Quarters station; I wouldn't have known what to do if I went to one. I was too damned young to realize what was going on. I didn't even know that this was a war breaking out. I thought this was just some big mistake that was being made.

Over the Side

But after the second or third bomb—I don't know which—that hit the *Arizona*, and after the second or third torpedo that hit—I can't remember to this day whether it was the explosions or sheer panic within me—I wound up over the side of the *Arizona* in the water. The *Arizona* was hit numerous times on the top deck and numerous times on the waterline with torpedoes. This is my recollection, and I don't say it's absolutely correct.

Like I say, to this day I ask myself whether it was the bomb explosions while I was on the top deck that knocked me over or whether it was the inner emotion that made me jump over. I would not be a bit abashed to admit if I jumped over, but I really don't remember. All I know is that the next thing I knew I was in the water. This is just a void, a blank, but I know after the second or third bomb, or it may have been the torpedoes, I was in the water.

> There were steel fragments in the air, fire, oil—God knows what all—pieces of timber, pieces of the boat deck, canvas, and even pieces of bodies.

I was fully clothed. Of course, I lost my cap when I went in. Man's desire for self-preservation is great. I swam away from the *Arizona* to the nearest mooring buoy. I hung on there for the balance of the attack. The buoy was astern of the *Arizona* and approximately twenty, twenty-five, or thirty yards away. It was approximately eight feet across and probably ten or fifteen feet deep. It had a lot of algae on it, green algae, barnacles, and everything. But I managed to get on the far side, and I did hang on—out of fear only. I was out of the water from a little above my waist. I was safer there than if I had been on the *Arizona* for the entire battle.

There were steel fragments in the air, fire, oil—God knows what all—pieces of timber, pieces of the boat deck, canvas, and even pieces of bodies. I remember lots of steel and bodies coming down. I saw a thigh and leg; I saw fingers; I saw hands; I saw elbows and arms. It's far too much for a young boy of fifteen years old to have seen. Of course, I never got hit by any of it. I didn't have a scratch when it was over with. I did have quite a bit of oil and sludge and diesel oil all over me. In fact, my white uniform didn't look white anymore; it was black.

Most of the fire was confined to the actual ship area, which was fifteen or twenty yards away. If I was in danger of catching afire, I didn't realize it. I saw a lot of fire, but it wasn't coming toward me. There was fire on the beach, too. I would have gone ashore, except there was so much havoc going on with the bombing at the naval air station on Ford Island, which was about three quarters of a mile away.

> The Japanese kept coming in constantly, wave after wave, and it seemed like they were completely uncontested, unmolested.

Watching from the Water

Now I was between a rock and a hard spot. I couldn't and I didn't want to go back to the *Arizona*, and from what was happening on Ford Island, I couldn't and didn't want to go there. So I was just more or less hanging on a thread for dear life.

All I can remember about this time is that the Japanese kept coming in constantly, wave after wave, and it seemed like they were completely uncontested, unmolested. I saw maybe one or two Jap planes that might have been hit and shot down. They were very low. After their bombing and torpedo runs, they came in strafing, but none was toward my area. They weren't paying any attention to me. Mainly they were going after the ships or anything of military value.

Photo on previous pages: The battleship USS *Arizona* toppled into the sea during the attack on Pearl Harbor on December 7, 1941. (Getty Images.)

I tell you, it was complete pandemonium. Like I said, I was too young at the time to fully realize what was going on, but I can describe it now thirty years later. It isn't the same at fifteen, but I've had time to dwell on it. It was a comedy of errors from the word "go!" The Navy was unprepared; none of the personnel had been trained for imminent attack. The ammunition wasn't readily available; damage control wasn't available; watertight hatches were never closed. Even though General Quarters sounded, most of the hatches never got closed. It was complete pandemonium.

I saw very few of our planes that got in the air. Most of them that I saw, looking over at Ford Island, had been bombed and set afire or blown apart. The ones that did get into the air were the real old-style planes. I can't remember if they were shot down or otherwise.

The *Arizona* finally started blowing up. There was ammunition, gun lockers, shells, steel fragments, and pyrotechnics coming from all parts of the ship. It was like a fireworks display. There was a series of explosions; it wasn't just one deafening roar. Things came to a final one where she seemed like the middle part just raised up in the water and kind of half buckled and then settled back down. Of course, she never sank, because the water at that time wasn't deep enough. Her bridge and masthead were above water; I remember that after that she finally settled. This was about the time when the attack was just about over. I decided to get the hell away from that mooring buoy.

I thought it was time to try to head for shore. I had to swim approximately three quarters to one mile to shore. I swam around the oil-covered water and then started toward Ford Island. The last incident I remember then during the attack is when I swam up on the island, which was rocky around the beach area there. The Marines were out on patrol, and everybody was trigger-happy because they thought of a possible invasion by the Japanese.

Here I was, in a white uniform, but it was more or less black. I had oil and sludge all over me. You couldn't have recognized that I was a white man.

I remember crawling ashore and running into a Marine sentry who wasn't much older than I, a year or two at most. Fortunately, the guy looked at me before he was ready to shoot. He thought I was a Japanese trying to come ashore. Only I screamed and hollered: "I'm Navy! I'm with the United States Navy! Don't shoot!" He didn't pull the trigger. But the rifle was aimed at me, and his finger was on the trigger.

Note

1. The [destroyer] *Shaw* was in the floating dry dock at the Navy Yard on December 7. She was badly damaged and later repaired. Matthews must have seen another ship destroyed. The minelayer *Oglala* was the only vessel sunk that could possibly have resembled the *Shaw*.

A Japanese American Citizen Describes Internment and His Decision to Join the Army

Minoru Masuda

In response to the attack on Pearl Harbor, President Franklin D. Roosevelt issued Executive Order 9066 on February 19, 1942, calling for the internment of Japanese Americans living on the West Coast of the United States. With this order, Japanese Americans, both citizens born in the United States and foreign nationals, were forced to leave their homes and businesses and relocate to isolated internment camps in inland areas of the country. What many government officials viewed at the time as a necessary step to ensure the country's security has since

SOURCE. Minoru Masuda, *Letters from the 442nd: The World War II Correspondence of a Japanese American Medic*. Seattle, WA: University of Washington Press, 2008. Copyright © 2008 by the University of Washington Press. All rights reserved. Reproduced by permission.

been reevaluated by many as rash and unjust. In the viewpoint that follows, Dr. Minoru Masuda, a second-generation Japanese American, recollects the day of the attack on Pearl Harbor, his time at two internment camps, and his eventual decision to enlist in the U.S. Army as a medic in the segregated, Japanese American 442nd Regimental Combat Team. The 442nd gained recognition and honor fighting in Europe. Dr. Masuda was a professor of psychiatry at the University of Washington.

I was born into the Japanese community in the heart of Chinatown, in Seattle. I grew up with it, was acculturated into it, and became a part of it. It was a bustling and hustling cohesive ethnic community, almost completely self-sustained, socially and economically. It had its own banks and a chamber of commerce, two Japanese-language newspapers, shops, fish markets, cleaners, hotels, restaurants, theaters, etc. The Nisei, my generation, the second generation, had its own English-language paper, its own athletic leagues, social functions, etc. In the thirties, then, it was an entirely different community than exists now, but this ethnic community was just as surely a ghetto as any other, even though not surrounded by stone walls. The community developed, as all immigrant communities do, because there was an internal need for people of a common language and custom and culture to band together in a strange land, and by doing so, they were buffered, isolated, and segregated, but protected from an alien, hostile, white American society. . . .

When Japan struck at Pearl Harbor on December 7, 1941, we were filled with anger and dismay at the turn of events. On that Sunday morning, a group of us had gone skiing at Paradise Valley on Mount Rainier and heard the news on the noon radio after a great morning run. At the shocking, incredible news, we gathered up and headed home, each of us sober and quiet, wondering what it all meant. Why had Japan done this stupid thing? What would happen to our parents? What would happen to all of us? It was a time for reflection and anxiety about what lay in store for all of us.

The Gradual Incarceration of Japanese Nationals

The FBI, from the evening of December 7, had begun to pick up and take away Japanese leaders in the community. In a matter of weeks, they had arrested dozens of our Japanese nationals—our Issei [first generation Japanese immigrants] parents. Japanese language-school teachers, business leaders, Buddhist priests, and organization heads were among those suspected to be disloyal and taken away.

I remember telling my father that since he was not a citizen—he couldn't become one even if he wanted to—he might be taken away as the others, but for him not to worry about the

> I said that we were American citizens, that we couldn't be touched, despite all the furor, because we were protected by the Constitution and the Bill of Rights.

family and the business (we ran a hotel in Japantown) because we—his sons—would keep the family and business together. I said that we were American citizens, that we couldn't be touched, despite all the furor, because we were protected by the Constitution and the Bill of Rights. I shall never forget what he said: "*Wakaranai yo*" ("I wouldn't be too sure"). Subsequent events were to prove that he had more wisdom than I in gauging the dark side of human nature.

Things were becoming more critical. Shortwave sections of our radios were removed. We turned in articles considered to be weapons. Curfew was imposed from 8:00 P.M. to 6:00 A.M. But the real blow was the promulgation of the presidential exclusion order in February 1942 [which allowed the internment of Japanese Americans]. Now we were thrust onto the track that eventually led to incarceration.

Reduced to a Number

It is strange, isn't it, and you will have to try somehow to understand this, how 110,000 people could so docilely and effectively organize themselves into being branded criminals and then to be led away to incarceration. . . .

My wife and I were reduced to a number—11704—as our identifying label. And with that label attached to our lapels, on that rainy morning in early May 1942, we took ourselves and what we could carry to Seventh and Lane streets to await the bus. And we were off to Puyallup, our temporary detention center.

> We lived, my wife and I, in Area B . . . a compound of long narrow barracks surrounding a central mess hall, toilet, shower, and laundry rooms, all enclosed by barbed wire six feet from the barrack walls.

Puyallup, our home until September, was the location of the Western Washington Fair. We had come to Puyallup—to these fair-grounds, to the wryly euphemistic "Camp Harmony"—stripped of our possessions, robbed of our dignity, degraded by epithets, and stigmatized as disloyal.

We lived, my wife and I, in Area B—in the parking lot to the east—a compound of long narrow barracks surrounding a central mess hall, toilet, shower, and laundry rooms, all enclosed by barbed wire six feet from the barrack walls.

Let me give you a short calendar of Camp Harmony events that I dug up from the *Minidoka Interlude* newspaper:

April 30   First movement from Seattle begins in the rain.

June 3   Western Defense Command orders nightly check-up of residents (just as you do at a prison).

July 4   July 4 celebration held in each area. Imagine celebrating Independence Day behind barbed wire!

July 13   War bond drive starts.

July 18   Japanese prints banned. Bibles and hymnals approved.

It is a bizarre mixture of events symbolical of patriotism and oppression.

Life in the Internment Camp

Life in Camp Harmony was the beginning of camp life that continued at Minidoka, Idaho [near the town of Hunt, about twenty miles from Twin Falls] in rattlesnake and sagebrush desert.

Minidoka was, like all the other nine concentration camps, located in the hinterlands, a prison set down in the swamps or desert where others would not live. Here the evacuees were to waste their lives for the duration—except for some students and workers, and those who went to war, some never to return.

The Minidoka Center rapidly became a self-organized community under the War Relocation Authority [WRA]—a civilian authority composed of human beings under Dillon Meyers. Previously the evacuation was under military control. It was the philosophy of the WRA to relocate the people out to jobs or schools, and it is to their credit that they had our welfare at heart under these circumstances when clearances were still an army function.

What can I tell you of Minidoka? We were assigned to Block 16, Barracks 5, Unit F at one end of a long tarpaper barrack. There it was—tiny, studs exposed, shiplap floor, dusty windows, two stacked canvas cots, a black potbellied stove sitting on a bed of sand, and a lightbulb hanging from the ceiling. We didn't even have a place to sit down and cry, except the floor.

My wife and I worked in the hospital, which was run by an Idaho physician, but the staff and personnel were all evacuees. My job was as a pharmacist; the pay was a professional group pay, the highest pay scale, nineteen dollars per month. In the late fall, we went out to work picking potatoes, and others went out to harvest sugar beets. We went to work for a Mennonite family—lived with them and worked with them—and they were very sympathetic and friendly. We got to know them well, went to their church and went into town on Saturday night, as did all the farmers there, and it was a very enjoyable stay away from camp.

> The physical hardships we could endure, but for me the most devastating experience was the unjust stigmatization by American society.

The Shame of Internment

The physical hardships we could endure, but for me the most devastating experience was the unjust stigmatization by American society, the bitter reminder that racism had won again over the Constitution and the Bill of Rights, the perception that the American people had thrown us into concentration camps simply because of our blood. It was galling, infuriating, and frustrating. Scapegoats we were, and imprisoned scapegoats to boot.

At the same time, the stigmatization of being branded disloyal and imprisoned evoked a sense of shame, as if the wrongful branding and the unjust act were somehow valid because of its sanction by American society, an upside-down perception.

Added to the self-imposed cloak of shame was the altogether human defense of submerging anger and bitterness: allowing it to surface and bubble would bring forth pain too strong to bear and detract from the goal of survival and achievement in the postwar years.

Serving a Country that Labels You a Traitor

Then, into this state of mind came the announcement that the army would be recruiting from the camp to form a segregated regimental combat team. The news fell like a clap of thunder on incredulous ears. How could the government and the army, after branding us disloyal, after stripping us of our possessions and dignity, and imprisoning us in barbed wire concentration camps, how could they now ask us to volunteer our lives in defense of a country that had so wrongfully treated us? The incredible announcement caused immediate turmoil and split the camp into two. One group reiterated the complete irrationality of the recruitment under these circumstances, and pointed out that once again the government was exploiting us and doing us in. The other group took the longer view and saw the threat posed to the future of the Nikkei if recruitment failed. A society as irrational and racist as the one that put us into Minidoka could as certainly be expected to follow by saying that the fact that there were no volunteers only proved their rightness in calling us disloyal and throwing us into camps.

I wrestled with the problem as both arguments tumbled around inside my head. It was a lonely and personal decision. I was older than the others. I was married, more mature, and had more responsibilities. It was a soul-searching decision, for the possibility of death in the battlefield was real, and, in the Nikkei context, almost expected. I admit, too, despite all the trauma, that an inexplicable tinge of patriotism entered into the decision to volunteer.

There were 308 volunteers for the 442nd Regimental Combat Team from the some six thousand to seven thousand people that were in camp.

The rest of the story is history: our induction, travel to Camp Shelby, Mississippi, our training with the larger Japanese American volunteer contingent from Hawaii, then overseas and the combat record of the 442nd.

CHRONOLOGY

1931
September 13   Japan invades Manchuria, China, and establishes the puppet state of Manchukuo the following year.

1937
July 7   Tensions between China and Japan escalate with the Marco Polo Bridge Incident, a battle between the Republic of China's National Revolutionary Army and the Imperial Japanese Army. The Japanese eventually overtake the bridge and invade Northern China.

1939
September 1   Germany invades Poland. Two days later Great Britain and France declare war on Germany.

1940
July   President Franklin D. Roosevelt signs the Export Control Act, allowing the president to limit or prohibit the exportation of war materials to Imperial Japan. Great Britain and Holland follow suit, imposing additional embargoes on Japan.

September 27   Germany, Italy, and Japan sign the Tripartite Pact allying the three countries as the Axis powers. Germany and Italy recognize and support Japan's imperialistic pursuits in Asia.

1941
January   Japanese naval general Isoroku Yamamoto first presents a plan to strike the United States in a preemptive attack on Pearl Harbor.

January 27	U.S. ambassador to Japan Joseph C. Grew sends a secret message to Washington, D.C., warning that Japan is considering making a surprise attack against the United States at Pearl Harbor. Believing an attack on U.S. assets in the Philippines is more likely, government officials disregard the message.
March 11	The "Lend-Lease" program between the United States and Great Britain begins with the U.S. pledging to give England and the Allied powers all the support they need "short of war." This agreement effectively ends the U.S. policy of neutrality in the war.
April 13	Japan and the Soviet Union sign the Soviet-Japanese Neutrality Pact to preserve security and peace between the two nations and end the Soviet-Japanese Border Wars as World War II and the Sino-Japanese War escalate.
July	President Roosevelt freezes Japanese assets in the United States and oil exports to Japan cease entirely. Again, Great Britain and Holland follow the U.S. lead.
November	Diplomatic relations between the United States and Japan become increasingly strained as the U.S. demands that Japan leave China and Indochina.
November 26	Thanksgiving Day. Japanese ships depart from the naval base in the Kurile Islands; twenty-four hours later, a cautionary message is sent to American military leaders in Hawaii, the Philippines, and the Panama Canal Zone that reads, "Consider this dispatch a war warning," alluding to the possibility of an attack on U.S. targets in the Pacific. Still, American officials consider the Philippines the likely target.
December 7	The first wave of Japanese planes strikes Pearl Harbor at 7:55 A.M. local time. Over the following two hours and

twenty minutes, Japanese aircraft and submarines inflict extreme damage on the naval and army bases in Hawaii, killing more than 2,400 U.S. troops and wounding another 1,200. The Japanese forces damage or destroy 18 ships and more than 300 aircraft. At the same time, Japanese forces begin their assault on the Philippines, Wake Island, and Guam.

December 8 President Roosevelt delivers the "Day of Infamy" speech and declares war against Japan, marking the United States' official entry into World War II.

1942
February 19 President Roosevelt signs Executive Order 9066 authorizing the designation of military zones on the west coast of the U.S. and the exclusion of certain or all individuals from these areas. As a result, individuals of Japanese ancestry are forced to abandon their homes, businesses, and lives in these regions and relocate to internment camps further inland. Sixty-two percent of the internees are U.S. citizens.

April 18 Lieutenant Colonel James Doolittle leads a carrier-launched air raid against military targets in Tokyo and surrounding cities. While the raid inflicts little damage on the targets, the assault, seen as retaliation for the Pearl Harbor attack, boosts American morale and shakes the leadership in Japan by proving that American forces could strike the Japanese home islands.

May 4–8 U.S. and Japanese carrier fleets meet at the Battle of the Coral Sea. While the Japanese won a tactical victory by sinking more and larger ships than they themselves lost, the Allied powers scored a strategic victory by averting the invasion of Port Moresby, which would have made the transfer of supplies between the U.S. and Australia difficult.

June 4–7   The Battle of Midway marks a turning point in the Pacific theater of war with the United States' decisive victory against the Japanese navy.

1943

February 1   Reversing an earlier decision prohibiting Japanese American men from serving, the U.S. Army forms a Japanese American combat unit—the 442nd Infantry.

April 18   Yamamoto, who led the attack against Pearl Harbor, is killed when U.S. army codebreakers notify the military of an intercepted message describing his movements; his plane is shot down en route to the Solomon Islands.

May   All U.S. naval vessels attacked at Pearl Harbor, except those sunk—the USS *Arizona, Utah,* and *Oklahoma*— are returned to active duty.

1944

June 6   D-Day commences when Allied troops storm the beaches of Normandy, France, in an effort to liberate Europe from Nazi forces.

December 16   The Battle of the Bulge begins in Belgium.

1945

January 25   The Allied victory at the Battle of the Bulge comes at a cost, with 800,000 soldiers participating and 19,000 U.S. troops killed, making it the largest and most deadly battle of the war for the United States.

April 30   Nazi leader Adolf Hitler commits suicide during the Battle of Berlin.

May 8   The Allied powers of World War II formally accept the surrender of the Nazis, commemorated as Victory in Europe Day or V-E Day.

August 6   The United States drops an atomic bomb on Hiroshima, Japan; between 90,000 and 160,000 people die during the blast and as a result of lingering radioactivity in the months that follow.

August 9   The United States drops an atomic bomb on Nagasaki, Japan; between 60,000 and 80,000 Japanese are killed that day and in the months following the blast.

August 15   Japan surrenders to the Allied powers.

September 2   The Pacific War—which began with Pearl Harbor—officially ends with the signing of the surrender document on the USS *Missouri* in Tokyo Harbor.

FOR FURTHER READING

Books

Harry Albright, *Pearl Harbor: Japan's Fatal Blunder: The True Story Behind Japan's Attack on December 7, 1941*. New York: Hippocrene, 1988.

Sadao Asada, *From Mahan to Pearl Harbor: The Imperial Japanese Navy and the United States*. Annapolis, MD: Naval Institute Press, 2006.

Paul S. Burtness and Warren U. Ober, eds. *The Puzzle of Pearl Harbor*. Evanston, IL: Row and Peterson, 1962.

Frank Chin, *Born in the USA: A Story of Japanese America, 1889–1947*. Lanham, MD: Rowman & Littlefield, 2002.

Thurston Clarke, *Pearl Harbor Ghosts: December 7, 1941, The Day that Still Haunts the Nation*. New York: Ballantine, 2001.

Hilary Conroy and Harry Wray, *Pearl Harbor Reexamined: Prologue to the Pacific War*. Honolulu: University of Hawaii Press, 1990.

David Ray Griffin, *The New Pearl Harbor Revisited: 9/11, the Cover-up, and the Exposé*. Northampton, MA: Oliver Branch, 2008.

Tameichi Hara, *Japanese Destroyer Captain: Pearl Harbor, Guadalcanal, Midway—The Great Naval Battles as Seen Through Japanese Eyes*. Annapolis, MD: Naval Institute Press, 1967.

David John Lu, *From the Marco Polo Bridge to Pearl Harbor: Japan's Entry into World War II*. Washington, DC: Public Affairs, 1961.

Martin V. Melosi, *The Shadow of Pearl Harbor: Political Controversy over the Surprise Attack, 1941–1946*. College Station, TX: Texas A&M University Press, 1977.

Edward S. Miller, *Bankrupting the Enemy: The U.S. Financial Siege of Japan Before Pearl Harbor*. Annapolis, MD: Naval Institute Press, 2007.

Frank P. Mintz, *Revisionism and the Origins of Pearl Harbor.* Lanham, MD: University Press of America, 1985.

Franklin Odo, *No Sword to Bury: Japanese Americans in Hawai'i During World War II.* Philadelphia: Temple University Press, 2004.

Gordon W. Prange, *At Dawn We Slept: The Untold Story of Pearl Harbor.* New York: Penguin, 1982.

Gordon W. Prange, *Pearl Harbor: The Verdict of History.* New York: McGraw-Hill, 1986.

Arthur William Radford, *From Pearl Harbor to Vietnam: The Memoirs of Admiral Arthur W. Radford.* Stanford, CA: Hoover Institution Press, 1980.

Emily S. Rosenberg, *A Date Which Will Live: Pearl Harbor in American Memory.* Durham, NC: Duke University Press, 2003.

James Rusbridger, *Betrayal at Pearl Harbor: How Churchill Lured Roosevelt into World War II.* New York: Summit, 1991.

Henry Dozier Russell, *Pearl Harbor Story.* Macon, GA: Mercer University Press, 2001.

Kazuo Sakamaki, *I Attacked Pearl Harbor.* New York: Association Press, 1949.

Alan Schom, *The Eagle and the Rising Sun: The Japanese-American War 1941–1943.* New York: W.W. Norton, 2004.

George Victor, *The Pearl Harbor Myth: Rethinking the Unthinkable.* Washington, DC: Potomac, 2007.

Bill Yenne, *Rising Sons: The Japanese American GIs Who Fought for the United States in World War II.* New York: Thomas Dunne, 2007.

Periodicals

Jim Adams, "Growing up with the Pearl Harbor Story," *Naval History*, December 2009.

Cliff Akiyama, "When You Look Like the Enemy," *Brief Treatment & Crisis Intervention*, May 2008.

Hanson W. Baldwin, "America at War: Three Bad Months," *Foreign Affairs*, April 1942.

Stephen Budiansky, "America, This Is London Calling: Before Pearl Harbor, the British Waged a Shrewd Propaganda War that Pulled a Country of Isolationists Into a Global Fight," *World War II*, May-June 2010.

Clarence E. Dickinson and Boyden Sparkes, "I Fly for Vengeance," *Saturday Evening Post*, October 10, 1942.

Otis L. Graham, "Fear Itself," *American Conservative*, February 23, 2009.

Mark Grimsley, "What If . . . Japan Hadn't Attacked Pearl Harbor?" *World War II*, September 2007.

Robert J. Hanyok, "The Pearl Harbor Warning that Never Was," *Naval History*, April 2009.

Frank E. Herrelko, Sr., "How I Remember Pearl Harbor," *Officer Review Magazine*, December 2008.

Humanities, "The War at Home," March-April 1995.

Warren Kozak, "A Japanese General Rewrites the Past," *Wall Street Journal*, December 5, 2008.

Amy Leinbach Marquis, "The Other Prisoners of War," *National Parks*, Spring 2007.

Nicolaus Mills, "Images of Terror," *Dissent*, Fall 2009.

Donald W. Mitchell, "Scapegoats and Facts," *Nation*, February 7, 1942.

John R. Murnane, "Japan's Monroe Doctrine?: Re-Framing the Story of Pearl Harbor," *History Teacher*, August 2007.

Norimistu Onishi, "Japan Fires General Who Said a U.S. 'Trap' Led to the Pearl Harbor Attack," *New York Times*, December 1, 2008.

Rachel Pfaff, "Attack on Pearl Harbor," *Current Events*, May 5, 2008.

L.E. Rogers, "Duel in the Rising Son," *Aviation History*, January 2010.

Saturday Evening Post, "Let's Forget Pearl Harbor," March 7, 1942.

Michael Shermer, "Paranoia Strikes Deep," *Scientific American*, September 2009.

Brian M. Sobel, "The 'Sacred Relics' of Pearl Harbor," *Wall Street Journal*, December 4, 2007.

I.F. Stone, "War Comes to Washington," *Nation*, December 13, 1941.

Barrett Tillman, "Into the Rising Son: The Doolittle Raid," *U.S. Naval Institute Proceedings*, April 2007.

Time, "Havoc at Honolulu," December 22, 1941.

Web sites

After the Day of Infamy (http://memory.loc.gov/ammem/ afcphhtml/afcphhome.html). This Library of Congress Web site presents a series of interviews conducted around the United States following the attack on Pearl Harbor. The responses of the participants present a first hand look at the atmosphere in the country in the days and months after the assault.

Confinement and Ethnicity: An Overview of World War II Japanese American Relocation Sites (www.nps.gov/ history/history/online_books/anthropology74/index.htm). This online book, presented by the National Park Service, chronicles the history of the Japanese American internment camps built in response to the attack on Pearl Harbor. Information about specific camps, as well as the justification given for internment, is all included.

Remembering Pearl Harbor (www.nationalgeographic.com/ pearlharbor). On this National Geographic site, visitors can explore the event in detail with an attack map, a minute-by-minute timeline of the attack, and a searchable archive of survivors' (both American and Japanese) stories.

World War II: Valor in the Pacific (www.nps.gov/valr/index .htm). This site is home of the Pearl Harbor Memorial and contains information about the USS *Arizona* Memorial as well as general information about the attack, including casualties, survivors' stories, and preservation information.

INDEX